The Magical Campus

Thomas Wolfe, 1919

The Magical Campus

UNIVERSITY OF
NORTH CAROLINA
WRITINGS

1917–1920

Thomas Wolfe

EDITED BY

Matthew J. Bruccoli and Aldo P. Magi

Foreword by Pat Conroy

THE UNIVERSITY OF SOUTH CAROLINA PRESS

© 2008 University of South Carolina
Foreword © 2008 Pat Conroy

Published by the University of South Carolina Press
Columbia, South Carolina 29208

www.sc.edu/uscpress

Manufactured in the United States of America

17 16 15 14 13 12 11 10 09 08   10 9 8 7 6 5 4 3 2 1

Library of Congress Cataloging-in-Publication Data

Wolfe, Thomas, 1900–1938.
    The magical campus : University of North Carolina writings, 1917–1920 / Thomas Wolfe ; edited by Matthew J. Bruccoli and Aldo P. Magi ; foreword by Pat Conroy.
        p. cm.
    Includes bibliographical references and index.
    ISBN 978-1-57003-734-4 (cloth : alk. paper)
    I. Bruccoli, Matthew Joseph, 1931– II. Magi, Aldo P. III. Title.
    PS3545.O337A6 2008
    813'.52—dc22
                            2007049939

In memory of my mentors,
Richard Walser and John S. Phillipson

A.P.M.

. . . it was as close to magic as I've ever been

Thomas Wolfe to Benjamin Cone,
July 27, 1929

Contents

ATTRIBUTIONS

Appendixes

ILLUSTRATIONS

FOREWORD

Pat Conroy

As I write these words, I have now lived twenty-four years longer on this immense and prodigal earth than the North Carolina writer Thomas Wolfe received as his stingy allotment of time. He died when he was thirty-seven years old and in the prime of his writing life. I have mourned for my entire adulthood that the world and I had stolen from us the novels Wolfe would have written in his forties, fifties, and sixties. When I first read *Look Homeward, Angel,* I was a sixteen-year-old boy living in the lowcountry of South Carolina. I told my mother that I planned to find and meet Wolfe that next summer, but my mother informed me that Thomas Wolfe had died long before I was born. I accepted this blow as part of my unlucky fate, then read *Look Homeward, Angel* straight through for a second time before I tackled that great doorstop and train ride of a second novel, *Of Time and the River.*

There has never been a boy in the history of the English-speaking world who was so Wolfe-possessed and Wolfe-besotted as I was. It causes me some discomfort to recall how indebted I am to his prodigious influence on my early writings, yet I am filled with eternal gratitude that he burst into the dead center of my life with the precipitous fierceness of thunderstorm. I was never the same boy again after I read *Look Homeward, Angel* and never, a single time, wanted to be. Thomas Wolfe, in his passionate fluency and exuberant generosity of spirit, had handed me the codes and passwords, written in invisible ink, about the troubled young man I was turning into without my consent or knowledge. He brought me grand tidings about who I was and what it was possible for me to turn myself into and handed over the understanding that literature could do anything. It was a gift of infinite price and one that I find awe inspiring and unrepayable. I was a writer from the day my magnificent English teacher, Eugene Norris, gave me a copy of Wolfe's first novel. But it took me years of squawking and chirruping and writing with an overwrought and dreadful intensity to discover this fact. My long apprenticeship began the day I finished *Look Homeward, Angel.* Having lived a longer life than he did, I now know something that Thomas Wolfe did not know when he died of tuberculosis of the brain in Baltimore in 1938. The apprenticeship of a writer is never over. It begins again every day of a writer's life with the merciless approach of the blank page, which is unfathomable and endless.

I would have profited greatly from reading *The Magical Campus: University of North Carolina Writings, 1917–1920* when I was in high school or during my four years at the Citadel. There is great value in studying the early writings and clumsy attempts of the writers who become famous for their artistry and mastery later in their lives. In this book we get to follow the young Thomas Wolfe's struggle to find his way in the poems, essays, articles, and plays he wrote while a student at his beloved University of North Carolina. Contained in this book are the first stirrings of Wolfe's compulsion to write, and they can be summed up in what the academics call, in their love of the Latinate putdown, juvenilia. But I found it an instructive thing to watch the awkwardness and unsurefootedness of Wolfe's early talent, the first inchoate cries of an ambitious young man eager to find his authentic voice, that one not yet fully born into the world. At Beaufort High School in 1962, I could have learned much from holding this book in my hand. I might have developed patience and constancy with myself as a writer instead of berating myself for writing sentences that were callow and flawed. The writings of Thomas Wolfe at Chapel Hill might have eased my own stormy self-loathing passage as an inept poet and short-story writer at the Citadel. It would have armed me with an abundance of hope when I began to set out on my own pallid voyages on the sea of English poetry and prose.

From this book you learn that it is the rare writer who springs fully formed and ready to tangle with those collisions and early impulses that stood guard between the writer and the first masterpieces. Wolfe, like all writers before and after him, learned that one has to produce acres of crabgrass and goldenrod and thistles before permission is granted to enter the greenhouse of art. Only years of practice, command, and failure grant you the right to cultivate those orchids to display before the world disguised as sentences of perfect order, beauty, and symmetry. This book proves that, as a college student, Thomas Wolfe had extraordinary talent and potential. It also proves that he was not yet Thomas Wolfe.

At the Citadel my devotional obsession with Thomas Wolfe made me something of a joke with my English professors. I wrote three essays about Wolfe for my freshman English class, which was taught by my faculty adviser, Colonel John Robert Doyle. In my sophomore year *Look Homeward, Angel* was the subject of my final speech of the academic year. The cadet who went before me gave his speech on the Battle of Cowpens. Several of my professors over the years told me they would cheerfully shoot the teacher who introduced me to the writings of Thomas Wolfe. Colonel John Carpenter, my Milton teacher, asked me if I ever encountered an adjective that did not cause me to "tremble with delight."

In my senior year I delivered a paper to the Calliopean Literary Society, the oldest club on campus, on Thomas Wolfe's entire body of work. I went to the generous-hearted Colonel Doyle and asked him if I could invite Thomas Wolfe's brother down to the Citadel to hear my talk and possibly talk about his famous sibling after I had finished. Colonel Doyle detested the writings of Wolfe but let me make the three-minute phone call to Wolfe's brother, who lived in Spartanburg. Though I could offer him room and board, I could not offer the fictional Luke Gant of *Look Homeward, Angel* a stipend for either his travel or his appearance at the Citadel. Thomas Wolfe's brother was charming and voluble and kind in his refusal, and I was delighted to be talking to the brother of my literary hero, who was also a fictional character in my favorite novel. Colonel Doyle had put his foot down hard when I tried to write my senior essay on Wolfe and directed me toward writers he thought possessed more restraint and a finer literary sensibility. The good Colonel Doyle was the first of many academics I have met who have pooh-poohed the merits of Wolfe's output. He desired that my critical attentions be directed toward Faulkner, Camus, or James Joyce. But I reminded Doyle in the unspeakable stubbornness of my last days as a cadet that I did not want to spend my whole life studying the properties of fire. Like Thomas Wolfe, I wanted to make that fire.

There are early works of Wolfe in *The Magical Campus* that I have waited my whole life to read. In the biography by his agent, Elizabeth Nowell, I had first read about the play *The Return of Buck Gavin: The Tragedy of a Mountain Outlaw,* which Wolfe had starred in when it was produced by the Carolina Playmakers. He had written it under the direction and influence of his charismatic teacher, Frederick Koch, who had recently arrived at Chapel Hill with a radical theory. It was his theory that a playwright should mine the folkways of North Carolinians for the raw materials that would animate the dramas that were the motherlode of every human life. In vain I had searched for a copy of *The Return of Buck Gavin,* and I never found one until I was sent the manuscript for this book. I read it with joy and nostalgia. It is not great, by any means, but it is a setting out and a beginning. I thought as I read through the college works of Thomas Wolfe that there is still nothing more indispensable or shaping or everlasting than a college education. I believe that *The Return of Buck Gavin* represented Wolfe's first ungainly baby steps, which would lead in an inexorable, unerring path to the publication of *Look Homeward, Angel* in 1929.

The youthful Wolfe takes great pleasure in his college career, and you can almost hear him chuckling at his attempts at humor, for which the adjective "sophomoric" seems perfect. When he writes poetry, you can feel how the obligations of form and rhyme handcuff a writer who would one day surrender to the oceanic surges and tidal pulls of a prose style unlike any other. The raw patriotism Wolfe displays in his college years is authentic and fierce and consistent with a nation caught up in the unimaginable carnage of World War I. It is fascinating to hear the German enemy referred to without apology as "The Hun," yet there are distant echoes that suggest Wolfe remains in the grip of that lingering romantic myth that still haunted the imaginations of all Americans after the terrible bloodletting of the American Civil War. The story "A Cullenden of Virginia" is an imaginary plight of a young soldier's courage failing him when the guns begin to roar in the trenches of France. It still reads like the diary of a young southern soldier dismayed by cannon fire loosening up the field of battle before the fearful assaults of Gettysburg or Antietam or the Wilderness. There is a prize-winning essay on the crisis of industry, and Wolfe dabbles in sports writing and satire and gives the impression that few men or women ever enjoyed their college days or got more out of them than he did.

When encountering the early prose of Thomas Wolfe, you cannot help but notice that you can always step into a rainforest of adverbs in his early stories and plays. I had a succession of superb English teachers who held strong and unsorrowful aversions to the poor adverb, and I have watched adverbs come under sustained assault from enemies as varied as the imperious Strunk and White to the less austere but equally disapproving Stephen King. The adverb seems to have encountered fewer archenemies in Wolfe's Chapel Hill world. You see his courtship of the bold and dazzling adjective begin to claim his youthful affections. Because of my Wolfe obsession, I read everything included in this book with avidity and interest. It made me pray that no one ever collects the crimes I committed against our pretty language while I was a Citadel cadet who wrote for the student magazine, the *Brigadier,* and the literary magazine, the *Shako.* But this book is indispensable to Wolfe scholars and a treasury to a man like me. Again I tell young writers there are worse ways to pursue a literary career than the one I chose. Out of hero worship and mimicry, I gave up my heart and soul to Thomas Wolfe. Because of this book, *The Magical Campus,* my long search for *Buck Gavin* has a happy ending. I always thought the title of Thomas Wolfe's *You Can't Go Home Again* was wrong. When I read the first pages of *Look Homeward, Angel,* I had come home at last, and it was Thomas Wolfe who threw me the key to the rest of my life.

PREFACE

Matthew J. Bruccoli

Thomas Wolfe matriculated at Chapel Hill in 1916 before his sixteenth birthday. He was obscure, unathletic, and lonely: "the greenest of all green freshmen, past and present" (*O Lost,* 428). He never became a jock; but by his junior year he was a prominent and popular campus figure, a brilliant student, and the star undergraduate writer/editor—as described through the autobiographical Eugene Gant:

> He was happier than he had ever been in his life, and more careless. His physical loneliness was more complete and more delightful. His escape from the bleak horror of disease and hysteria and death impending that hung above his crouched family, left him with a sense of aerial buoyancy, drunken freedom. He had come to the place alone, without companions. He had no connections. He had even now not one close friend. And this isolation was in his favor. Everyone knew him at sight; everyone called him by name, and spoke to him kindly. He was not disliked. He was happy, full of expansive joy, he greeted everyone with enthusiastic gusto. He had a vast tenderness, an affection for the whole marvelous and unvisited earth that blinded his eyes. He was closer to a feeling of brotherhood than he had ever been, and more alone. He was filled with a divine indifference for all appearance. Joy ran like a great wine through his young expanding limbs; he bounded down the paths with wild cries in his throat, leaping for life like an apple, trying to focus the blind desire that swept him apart, to melt down to a bullet all of his formless passion, and so, slay death, slay love.
>
> He began to join. He joined everything. He had never "belonged" to any group before, but now all groups were beckoning him. He had without much trouble won a place for himself on the staff of the college paper and the magazine. The small beginning trickle of distinctions widened into a gusher. It began to sprinkle, then it rained. He was initiated into literary fraternities, dramatic fraternities, theatrical fraternities, speaking fraternities, journalistic fraternities, and in the spring into a social fraternity. He joined enthusiastically, submitted with fanatical

glee to the hard mauling of the initiations, and went about lame and sore, more pleased than a child or a savage, with colored ribbons in his coat lapel, and a waistcoat plastered with pins, badges, symbols, and Greek letterings. (*O Lost,* 523)

Wolfe's ascendancy to the editorship of the *Tar Heel* was in part attributable to the departure of the staff for military service in World War I—for which he was too young: "He Carried On. He Held High the Torch. He Did His Bit. He was editor, censor, factotum of the paper. He wrote the news. He wrote the editorials. He seared them with flaming words. He extolled the crusade. He was possessed of the inspiration of murder" (*O Lost,* 577).

Wolfe had two one-act plays produced by the Carolina Playmakers. The American writers who served their literary apprenticeships at college typically did so by neglecting their studies: F. Scott Fitzgerald is the classic case of a young writer who regarded required courses as a waste of time. Wolfe was a serious student, although his classroom performances were more impressive than his grades.

The peak of Wolfe's college recognition came when Professor Horace Williams awarded him the Worth Prize as a junior for *The Crisis in Industry*—his first separately published work. This achievement inspired a scene in *O Lost* that was cut from *Look Homeward, Angel:*

As he went up the path he heard the mellow class bell ringing jubilantly. Then the son of the registrar, Billy Watson, bounded down the broad stone steps of Faculty Hall and ran towards him with high leaping stride.

"What are the bugles blowing for?" said Eugene.

"You've made the first One that Vergil Weldon has given in Logic for eighteen years!" screamed Billy Watson. "And your essay has won the Ramsay Prize. It will be published."

Then other boys rushed at him from all sides, yelling: "You made a One on Logic, 'Gene!"

"O Christ! O God!" Eugene screamed, casting his arms up. "I feel so good I could die!" (*O Lost,* 628–29)

Wolfe's senior year photograph and record of student activities. From *Yackety Yack,* 1920. North Carolina Collection, University of North Carolina at Chapel Hill

THOMAS CLAYTON WOLFE
ASHEVILLE, N. C.
Age, 19; Weight, 178; Height, 6 feet 3 inches

Di Society; Buncombe County Club; Freshman-Sophomore Debate (2); Dramatic Association; Carolina Playmakers (3, 4), Author two One-Act Plays, Executive Committee (4); Associate Editor YACKETY YACK (3); Associate Editor *Magazine* (3), Assistant Editor-in-Chief (4); Managing Editor *Tar Heel* (3), Editor-in-Chief (4); Advisory Board *Tar Baby* (4); Worth Prize in Philosophy (3); Y. M. C. A. Cabinet (3, 4); Student Council (4); Athletic Council (4); Class Poet (3, 4); Chairman Junior Stunt Committee; German Club; Amphoterothen; Satyrs; Golden Fleece.

Σ Υ; Ω Δ; Π Κ Φ.

EDITING the *Tar Heel,* winning Horace's philosophy prize when only a Junior, writing plays and then showing the world how they should be acted—they are all alike to this young Shakespeare. Last year he played the leading role in the "Midnight Frolic" at "Gooch's Winter Palace", but this year it's the leading role on the "Carolina Shipping Board". But, seriously speaking, "Buck" is a great, big fellow. He can do more between 8:25 and 8:30 than the rest of us can do all day, and it is no wonder that he is classed as a genius.

"AW! BUCK, WHY DIDJA DO IT?"

Acknowledgments

The familiar acknowledgment that "this book would not have been published without the help of . . ." is usually exaggerated. Nonetheless this book would not have been published without the encouraging support of Nicholas Graham, head of Public Services, Wilson Library, University of North Carolina, Pulpit Hill. The Houghton Library, Harvard University, is consistently helpful. We are also much obligated to Jo Cottingham, head of Inter-Library Loan, Thomas Cooper Library, University of South Carolina; Jill Jividen, research assistant, Department of English, University of South Carolina; Carol Cheschi, Bruccoli Clark Layman; and Judith S. Baughman, Department of English, University of South Carolina. Steven Lynn, chairman, Department of English, University of South Carolina, provided aid and comfort. We are also grateful to David J. Wyatt, Hinckley, Ohio, for providing us with research materials.

M.J.B.

A.P.M.

Wolfe's Editorial Positions

The *Tar Heel*
Assistant editor: October 2, 1918
Managing editor: October 9, 1918–June 14, 1919
    Editor Forrest Miles was away November 22–December 20, 1918; Wolfe
    moved to top of masthead as managing editor
Editor-in-chief: October 11, 1919–June 5, 1920

The *Magazine*
Assistant editor: April 1919
Assistant editor-in-chief: December 1919, February 1920, April 1920

The *Tar Baby*
Editor of the April 10, 1920, issue

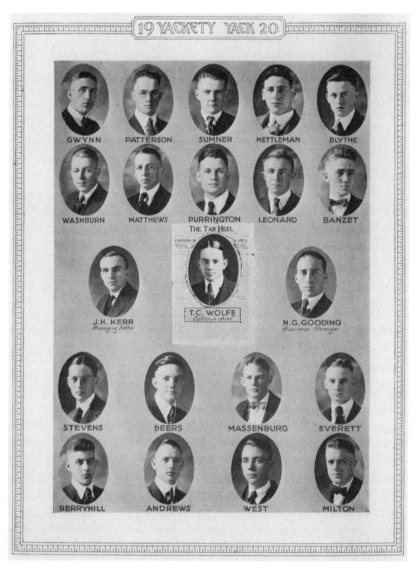

Tar Heel staff, 1919–20. From *Yackety Yack,* 1920. North Carolina Collection, University of North Carolina at Chapel Hill

SIGNED PUBLICATIONS

"A Field in Flanders," 1917

University of North Carolina Magazine, November 1917, 77

Thomas Wolfe did not submit his work to the *University of North Carolina Magazine* until his sophomore year at Chapel Hill. The three-stanza poem "A Field in Flanders," the first of four poems and a short story infused with patriotic fervor, is considered Wolfe's first published writing. In "Writing and Living" (in *The Autobiography of an American Novelist,* edited by Leslie Field [Cambridge: Harvard University Press, 1983], 105), a speech he delivered at Purdue University a few months before his death, Wolfe recalled this poem "about a peasant in a Flanders field who ploughed up a skull, and then went on quietly about his work, while great guns blasted far away."

A.P.M.

A Field in Flanders

THOMAS WOLFE

The low, grey clouds are drifting 'cross the sky,
    While here and there the little smoke puffs break,
And now and then the shrapnel bursts on high,
    And growling guns their mighty thunder make.

A war-ripped field,—with what a tale to tell!
    A tale to cause the souls of kings to quake,
For here, within a smoking, bloody Hell,
    Ten million risk their lives for Freedom's sake.

And to the right a ruined village burns,
    And to the left a wood its secrets hold,
But in the gutted field the plowshare turns
    A grinning skull which sneers its message bold.

The
University of North Carolina
Magazine

Old Series Vol. 48   No. 2   New Series Vol. 35

CONTENTS FOR NOVEMBER, 1917

Wolfe's first publication in the university literary journal. North Carolina Collection, University of North Carolina at Chapel Hill

"To France," 1917

University of North Carolina Magazine, December 1917, 165

Wolfe's second appearance in the university magazine came a month after "A Field in Flanders." Like its predecessor and the three works to follow, "To France" is a tribute to the brave men who fought and sacrificed their lives for the noble cause of democracy and freedom in the Great War.

A.P.M.

To France

THOMAS WOLFE

O France, you truly are sublime,
    The thought of you shall make men thrill
Throughout all ages and all time.
    Your story lives and ever will.

When Huns came down with bloody hand,
    And left fair Belgium desolate,
Up bravely from their peaceful land
    Rushed strong defenders of thy state.

They fought until all hope seemed gone,
    Without a groan—without a sigh.
And still brave France kept fighting on
    Until it seemed that France must die.

Oh France, to you who never feared,
    To you who nobly stood the test,
With blazing eyes and plumes upreared,
    The eagle comes from out the West.

"The Challenge," 1918

University of North Carolina Magazine, March 1918, 223

Wolfe's third poem, "The Challenge," one among an array of patriotic pieces in the March 1918 issue of the university magazine, was written in the style and meter of James Russell Lowell's antislavery poem "The Present Crisis." In "Writing and Living," Wolfe later recalled that the poem "was aimed directly at the luckless head of Kaiser Bill." Wolfe also noted that he referred to the kaiser as "thou dog" but that "the more conservative element on the editorial staff felt that the words . . . jarred rudely upon the high moral elevation of the poem. . . . Above my own vigorous protest, they were deleted" (104).

In *Thomas Wolfe Undergraduate* (Durham, N.C.: Duke University Press, 1977), Richard Walser states, "It was not 'A Cullenden of Virginia' but 'The Challenge' which brought Wolfe a sudden burst of fame" (45). The poem was reprinted in Wolfe's hometown newspaper, the *Asheville Citizen* (April 5, 1918), and elsewhere in the South.

A.P.M.

The Challenge

THOMAS WOLF [*sic*]

You have given us your mandates,—we have made our purpose clear,
We will buy the prize with red blood and no price will be too dear,
We will pay the price with manhood,—with the smoke from cannons curled,
Until Freedom stands unchallenged with her banners to the world.

We have spoken,—you have heard us,—there can be no middle way,
The despot hurls his challenge,—he extends his iron sway,
Now the time has come to reckon,—we protect with sword and lance,
The stars and bars of Freedom, the tri-color of brave France.

Look, ye tyrant, look and tremble, let your heart with fear be filled,
At that principle of nations which a dormant world has thrilled,
See,—our legions come to meet you, and their cause is pure and right,
With one purpose, all united, mighty armies come to fight.

History, the great Exemplar, shows us well those nations' path,
Those who leave their altars holy, cannot feel a righteous wrath.
By this token shall we profit,—we who know, shall different be,
Nation answers unto nation,—mighty hands grip o'er the sea.

You, proud ruler, made the challenge, we have answered all in all,
Aye, we answered with all gladness, for we heard a great creed's call
To a war that is our cleanser—one that keeps us from decay,
One that makes for future freedom:—we are in our own to-day.

We have taken up the gauntlet,—we will answer blow for blow,
You have sent your blood and iron, pay thou then the cost, and go.
All our hearts are filled with glory at the wonder that will be,—
We have taken up the gauntlet and, thank God, men shall be free.

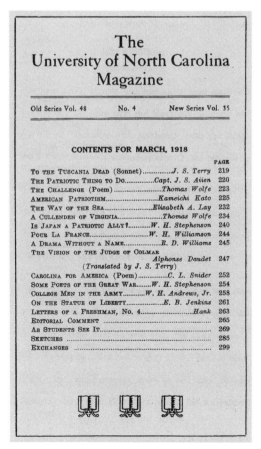

North Carolina Collection,
University of North Carolina
at Chapel Hill

The University of North Carolina Magazine

Old Series Vol. 48   No. 4   New Series Vol. 35

CONTENTS FOR MARCH, 1918

"A Cullenden of Virginia," 1918

University of North Carolina Magazine, March 1918, 234–39

"A Cullenden of Virginia" is Wolfe's first published work of fiction. In "Writing and Living" he recalled his story "about the recreant son of an old family who recovers his courage, and vindicates his tarnished honor in the last charge over the top that takes his life" (105). In the *Tar Heel* (March 23, 1918), R. R. Thornton, professor of journalism, noted that Wolfe's short story resembled Guy de Maupassant's story about a coward and observed that Wolfe's "two contributions to this issue give promise that he is to do much excellent work in the future. He writes well and with much imaginative insight."

A.P.M.

A Cullenden of Virginia

THOMAS WOLFE

Four o'clock was zero hour. It [was] now three-thirty and out across the bleak, level land, gutted with shell pits and craters, the sky was becoming a pale, cold grey. All was silent, the guns had hushed their angry growling and were still. Both armies lay gripped in the ominous silence that precedes the attack.

To Roger Cullenden, waiting in his trench, it seemed that anything was preferable to this terrible, oppressive silence. It pounded on his ears with a thunder louder than that of the cannon. He felt that he must scream. His mind seemed unable to focus on any detail and, curiously enough, little absurd occurrences of his boyhood kept flashing back to him. These trivialities came flooding in and, rather helplessly, he wondered why. At intervals he would think of the impending attack, and then, it seemed his bones turned to water and his blood froze with the horror of the thought. He wondered desperately if he were a coward. He kept repeating over and over again to himself: "Good God! A Cullenden of Virginia a coward!"

Cullenden's father had fought in the Civil War, his grandfather in the Mexican War, and his great-grandfather in the War of 1812, and so on back as far as people could remember the name of the Cullendens of Virginia had come to be synonymous not only with the flower of aristocracy, but even more so with personal bravery. It had been but the natural, traditional thing for the present Cullenden Senior, when America entered the World War in 1917, to grasp his son by the hand, look straight into his eyes and tell him to go. Roger Cullenden went gayly, heedlessly, thoughtlessly,—going to war as he had gone about everything else in his care-free life.

All these things came crowding back as he crouched there in his trench, gazing unseeingly at his wrist watch with mechanical regularity. He was overwhelmed with a kind of weak self-pity and he suddenly felt a hot splash in his hand and realized that he was snuffling audibly. He cursed himself as a weak fool. Perhaps you can excuse Cullenden. He had been in the trenches only two weeks. It was his first experience of modern warfare. And then, too, he was only a boy.

Cullenden was cursed with an almost too vivid imagination. The day before a sentry had been careless enough to give the Boche snipers a fair shot at his head. And now, as Cullenden thought of the dead man and the gob of gore and brains where his head had been, he became very sick. He muttered: "God! Suppose I should get it like that!" And again he leaned against the walls of the trench overcome with the horror of it.

Once more he glanced at his wrist watch. Ten minutes to four. He looked around curiously to see how his companions were taking it. Some talked jerkingly to each other in a shaking voice. Others tried to give the impression of extreme calmness. One man was seated on a keg, apparently absorbed in a newspaper and puffing away vigorously on a pipe. Cullenden thought it rather strange that the newspaper was upside down and that the pipe had no tobacco in it. The young lieutenant walked among his men trying vainly to impart a cheerfulness that he himself was far from feeling. With a hand that shook, he consulted his wrist watch every half minute. The minutes seemed as hours to Cullenden waiting, waiting, waiting.

One minute to four. Cullenden thought he was stifling. He tried desperately to regain some part of his accustomed calm but it was no use. A whistle blew. A lieutenant in a cheery but rather falsetto voice quavered: "All up, men, let's go over, all together." At the same time, with a titanic crash, the barrage started and the ground trembled to the mighty roar of the big guns. By a supreme effort Cullenden dragged himself over the top of the trench and started out at a walk. The enemy machine guns were raking all along the line, doing their nasty work. The man beside him gave a funny little cough and crumpled up. Cullenden felt sick. The lieutenant was walking about thirty feet in front of him when a shrapnel shell burst squarely over his head. Cullenden felt himself drenched with the warm dew. His strained nerves could stand no more, and he yielded to the devil that tormented him. He flung himself, with a moan of terror, into a slight depression caused by a shell and pillowed his face in his hands. Then the sickening realization of what he had done swept over him. He,—a Cullenden of Virginia,—was a coward! Good God! What would people say?

Beyond him he heard faintly the sound of cheering. They had beaten Fritz out of his section of the first line trenches. His company would miss him soon, no doubt. They would think him wounded, while he lay here untouched! What would they say when they found him here? He would be disgraced. Think of the pain to his father, the disappointment of his friends. Cullenden thought most of his friends.

His mind flashed back to his college years. The dim, gray wraiths of the past began to come forth and remind him of his shame. One by one he recalled them—his friends—all in the service now—he knew not where—save only one of them—Johnny Millard. He had been his "alter ego" all during their four years of college. When Cullenden had enlisted, Johnny had enlisted with him, in order that they might fight the Hun together. And then some perverse fate had separated them. Dear old Johnny—where was he now? . . .

As Cullenden thought of these a new fear seized him, more potent than any he had yet known. It was a different fear. He was afraid of being thought afraid and, compared to this fear, mere physical fear could be easily borne. He thought of his father and uttered a groan. The disgrace would, he knew, well nigh kill the proud, sensitive old man.

Frantically he cudgelled his brain for some loop-hole. Then, suddenly, the evil impulse flashed upon him. They thought him dead or wounded. Well, then, why not be wounded? Slowly his hand moved along the ground and gripped the stock of his gun.

———

For thirty minutes now the attack had raged. The great guns still roared their mighty thunder. The spitting fire of machine guns could be heard between explosions, shrieks, yells—everything in fact, that went to make up a red inferno. The second wave of the attack had just gone by, their figures looming darkly in the mist of early morning.

It was time for the third wave. A hazy line of figures advanced at a steady dog trot and passed over the place where Cullenden lay watching. But the Fritzies were doing wicked work with their machine guns. The line thinned perceptibly. A stocky figure came trotting up, stopped, whirled, as if meeting with some sudden impact and fell near the spot where Cullenden lay. Cullenden cursed, for he had been on the verge of pulling the trigger.

The wounded man heard him. He raised himself painfully on his elbow and said in cheerful tone: "What's the matter, friend? Did they get you too?"

He looked at Cullenden's face a moment with dawning recognition, then burst forth: "Well, I'll be damned, Roger Cullenden!"

The man in the shell hole turned ashen. There could be only one voice in the world like that. He looked at the injured man closely. Beneath the accumulation of trench dirt, beneath a three weeks growth of beard, were the smiling features of Johnny Millard. The unbelievable had happened.

Johnny was saying with forced cheerfulness: "Nothing much wrong with me, old top. I got it through the leg. About six weeks in hospital will do for me, I guess. But tell me," anxiously, "where did they get you?"

Cullenden stuttered through white lips: "I—I—I," then dropped his head and was silent. Millard looked for a moment with a puzzled expression. "What's the matter, Roger? Why don't you answer? Why—" Then, all at once, the truth burst on his astounded senses. Disbelief, pain, anger were all mingled on his countenance. He clinched his hands convulsively and then he thought of how over there American boys—Americans with good red blood in their veins are giving it, while here lay his friend, a sneaking coward, lying faking. His friend, a Cullenden,—a descendant of fighting men. He wanted to say something. He tried, but his voice trailed off and ended in a sob.

With a terrible effort Cullenden raised his head. His face was chalk white and his eyes were terrible. They looked as if they had seen death.

However, he merely said in an unemotional voice: "Johnny," then his voice broke. "Johnny, everything you think is true and even that doesn't half express the whole truth. Do you know what I was about to do when you came up? Well, I was about to wound myself to save my face. Yes, I am everything you think and more. Good God!" His voice was high-pitched, hysterical.

But Johnny didn't hear the last. He had fainted from shock and loss of blood. Cullenden roused himself, went to where his friend lay and examined the wound. A nasty flesh stab, he saw, that required immediate attention. He never hesitated, but lifted the wounded man up in his arms and started back towards his trench. He had not gone far when a bursting shell reminded him that this ground, no longer covered by the barrage, was open to enemy fire. To go on meant almost certain death. Cullenden knew further that the field would be peppered by the enemy machine guns. But he never faltered, although by now the steel jackets were whining around him.

Cullenden was not afraid now. He had gone beyond fear—despair was now the only state his mind could know. Far away he heard the sound of cheering in the trenches. He knew it was for him—that down there men were hoping, praying for his safety—that men were watching with bated breath. He swallowed the lump in his throat. If they only knew the truth—the truth! He stumbled upon a machine gun emplacement, then pushed onward. Just three yards more and he had made it! As he reached the parapet of the trench, a white hot pain seared his lungs. He collapsed with his load. He knew, then, that he had gotten "it." Eager hands below dragged the two men into the trench.

Roger Cullenden slowly opened his eyes. A great red stain was slowly dying his shirt. He looked around at the little group that had formed about him. There was not one on whose face respect and admiration was not depicted. Thank God! They would never know the truth. What a fool—a cowardly fool—he had been! With a mighty effort he raised himself and looked at the sad faces around him. "Well, boys," he smiled, "They got me—got me good. But"—almost inaudible—"I am going out a Cullenden—of—Virginia." Slowly, flickeringly, his eyelids closed. Thirty seconds later he was dead.

"To Rupert Brooke," 1918

University of North Carolina Magazine, May 1918, 314–15

Poet Rupert Brooke (1887–1915), whom William Butler Yeats proclaimed "the handsomest young man in England," was born at Rugby and educated at Cambridge. He died of blood poisoning at Skyros during the Dardanelles expedition of World War I.

"To Rupert Brooke" was later privately printed in one hundred copies by the Lecram Press (Paris, 1946). The four Great War poems, along with "A Cullenden of Virginia," are reprinted in *Thomas Wolfe: A Documentary Volume,* Dictionary of Literary Biography Series, vol. 229, ed. Ted Mitchell (Detroit: Bruccoli Clark Layman / Gale, 2001). They were also published as *Thomas Wolfe and the Great War: Contributions to the University of North Carolina Magazine, 1917–1919* (Columbia: Joseph M. Bruccoli Great War Collection, Thomas Cooper Library, University of South Carolina, 2005).

A.P.M.

To Rupert Brooke

THOMAS WOLFE

I know of one whose name shall never die,—
Who has hurled forth his soul's immensity
In one fire blazoned passage that will live
"As long as we have wit to read and praise to give,"
And by this burning sentence from his hand:
"There is a spot that is forever England."

By just this thought, I say, he's made a name so dear
That closer it shall grow each passing year
To English hearts; it was a blazing thought.
He had the spark,—he lived and loved and wrought
And poured in one short verse his whole heart's treasure,
Then, daring all, dared give the "last full measure."

When all which is has fáded from men's thought,—
When we're forgotten,—our labors set at naught,—
When all to-day is gone,—then men will feel with joy
The written spirit of an English boy
Who died as he lived,—unpraised, unknown,
Unconscious of the mighty seed he'd sown.

When that is gone which men call everything,—
Our wretched aims,—the plots of marshal and of king,
His name will live. I would I could express
His beauty, truth and loveliness.
But I (and you) can only wonder when we read
The mighty love that's written here; for this his people bleed.

An age may silent be but for one Voice
That speaks its mighty travail. O rejoice
That even one to every age can be
Who has the latent spark, the eye to see,
The kindling heart by deep emotion fired,
The will to write that by the mind inspired.

If all were gone which the immortals gave,
How wretched would we live,—how like the slave!
They're sent to us at scattered times,—they speak Eternity,
We madly trample under foot the flower we never see,—
The flower that blooms amongst us, buds and blooms, and then
Bursts forth in glorious sweetness for all the race of men.

"The Drammer," 1919

Magazine, April 1919, 72–73

Wolfe began his junior year at Chapel Hill with the ambition to become fully engaged in campus activities. He was gratified by the invitation to become an assistant editor of the *Tar Heel,* and a week later he was appointed managing editor. A few months later he was chosen to be on the staff of the university's *Magazine* as an assistant editor. "The Drammer" is a parody of an old-fashioned melodrama with a despicable villain who takes advantage of a helpless damsel in distress.

At the time "The Drammer" was published, Wolfe was one of seven juniors tapped for membership in the Golden Fleece, the highest honor at the university. His wit, intelligence, and satirical sense of humor blended with his gregarious personality and engendered his reputation as a "big man on campus." He approached his newfound role with gusto.

A.P.M.

The Drammer

THOMAS WOLFE

> I love to view the passing show
> For that is where true art is,
> And surely modern writers know
> Just where our modern heart is.
>
> Last night I looked upon a play
> That fully won my favor;
> A melodrama, by the way,
> Of blood and thunder flavour.
>
> And lest you think the program tame,
> Meet: "Violet! the Prairie Rose!
> The fairest lily-flower that grows!"
> For this is all her program-name.

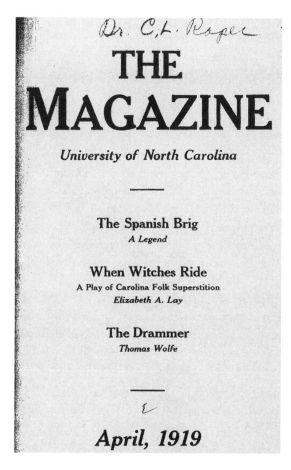

Front cover of the university magazine. North Carolina Collection, University of North Carolina at Chapel Hill

Then Desmond, deep-dyed vaudevillian,
The hero's chieftest hater,
(Hero's a rising aviator)
But Desmond drops him—this is killin'.
(ACT I, SCENE 1. EXIT HERO ON STRETCHER)

Mary was on concealment bent
From Desmond bold who wooed her,
But everywhere that Mary went
The villian there pursued her.

In vain she scorned her suitor's suit
He reaches out and nabs her
(ACT I, SC. 2)

And when with scorn she spurns the brute,
The scoundrel ups and stabs her.
(END ACT I)

And now we see a towering cliff
(ACT II, SC. 1)
Below a railway trestle,
In agony we wonder if
He'll do it—And they wrestle.
(ACT II, SC. 2)

Behold below!—a speeding train
He sees—th' plot is thick'ning,
She fights for life with might and main
But falls—the thud is sickening.
(END ACT II)

Now lo! We see wild Yukon chaps
(ACT III, SC. 1)
And Mary—what's her motive?
(A little tired and pale, perhaps,
From the weight of the locomotive.)

She's safe!—no!—Desmond knows no pity,
He looks for Mary far and near;
He tracks her from the teeming city
Until he finds her hiding here.
(ACT III, SC. 2)

He looks and laughs with fiendish note;
We really could berate him;
And when he chokes her fair white throat
We certainly could hate him.
(ACT III, SC. 2, STILL)

He chokes her till she gasps for breath,
He chokes her fair white throat, alas,
The rascal yet will be her death;
Why should things come to such a pass!

"An Appreciation," 1919

Magazine, May 1919, 79

Wolfe's whimsicality was evident in this piece of lighthearted verse that Richard Walser in *Thomas Wolfe Undergraduate* described as "a spurt of humor on the Japanese longing to be home in cherry-blossom time" (79). Wolfe used his first and middle names, Thomas Clayton, as the byline for this work. Subsequently he also used T. C. Wolfe and Thomas Clayton Wolfe for contributions to campus publications.

A.P.M.

An Appreciation

THOMAS CLAYTON

All Japs, he says, are poets then,
    When blossoms bloom in old Japan;
Ah! this is common to all men
    When blossoms bloom—since time began.

And he is far away from home
    And crudely, rudely tries to write
Of something that he feels so deep
    Of old Japan, where blossoms keep
Their vigil, blossoms far from sight
    In old Japan across the foam.

Now would you wonder if I said
    My eyes got bleary when I read
This little story of the Springtime
    That comes so whitely to Japan,
The joyous, smiling, rustling spingtime
    That brings fond mem'ries to the man?

"The Creative Movement in Writing," 1919

Tar Heel, June 14, 1919, 2

In the closing weeks of his junior year, at a final gathering of the student body on June 6, 1919, Wolfe read a paper extolling the creative work by students producing original poems, plays, and stories in courses taught by Frederick Koch, who founded the Carolina Playmakers Association, as well as work in Edwin Greenlaw's English literature courses. He praised these teachers for encouraging students to use their past experiences in their literary efforts: "Our men here are writing about that which they have experienced, and they are creating real stuff." Wolfe cited work accomplished in Koch's playwriting course in depiction of "folk lore and life traditions of North Carolina" and the work on "The Peace Treaty" for Greenlaw's class. He also praised Greenlaw's students, who were devoting their efforts "to the production of a novel dealing with the labor problem in a typical American community." He recognized their progress in completing "two books of this three-book novel." This novel was not published and has not been located.

Wolfe, who lacked athletic ability, concluded, "It may not be our lot, in our lives here at Carolina, to take part in the more spectacular activities of our college life, in athletics. But if we are not naturally endowed with athletic requirements, if we may not go out on the football field and cover ourselves with mud and glory,—remember: They also serve who only sit and write."

"The Creative Movement in Writing" is Wolfe's only bylined appearance in the *Tar Heel.*

A.P.M.

The Creative Movement in Writing

Men are doing much better writing on this campus than ever before in our university's history. It is not the writer's purpose to analyze this movement,—to find and state its causes.

The reason, we think, is fairly obvious. Ten, or even five years ago, the general criticism against college writers and their writing was not so much against its technique and style as against the content. The college men, as a rule, simply had nothing to write about.

But the college men of Carolina have passed through a great adventure and it is inconceivable that, after what they have seen and felt, they should still have nothing to write about. This is manifestly the reason for the new standard.

The literary work of the students on this campus this year has not been sporadic,—it has assume[d] well-defined proportions as a definite creative movement. Creative! That expresses it! Our men here are writing about that which they have experienced, and they are creating real stuff. The success of this new movement is more than gratifying.

Perhaps the most distinctive work that has been done in this line, is the work done under the auspices of the newly-formed Carolina Playmakers Association,—that most unique, but democratic organization which had its inception and is being directed by Prof. F. H. Koch, late of the University of North Dakota, where he directed a similar organization.

The purpose of the Playmakers Association is, briefly put, the production of original folk-dramas, dealing with the lives of Carolina folk. These plays are written by members of the new Dramatic Literature course, taught by Professor Koch; this course is part of the Playmakers Organization.

Let us consider the tremendous possibilities of this dramatic movement. These plays depend on the folk lore and life traditions of North Carolina. Upon its richness depends much of the success of this movement. There is, obviously, no part of the country more widely endowed with diversified character types or with varied folk traditions than our own North State. A drama that draws its production from such a source must be real stuff; it comes directly from the hearts and lives of the people. When we consider that the folk-drama has been one of the most important influences in humanizing the world; when we see the tremendous influence it had over Greek civilization, we may get some idea of the importance of this new movement.

Perhaps that explains the almost amazing success of Playmakers Association this year. Given its birth at a time when the normal activity of our college life was wholly deranged by the S. A. T. C., it has produced in two short semesters, five separate one-act productions, and is preparing to repeat two of these productions this Commencement week. It is not the writer's purpose to comment upon the success of these plays. Suffice it to say that critical but favorable comments have appeared in two New York dailies, in the Baltimore Sun, which also carried cuts of the productions along with a feature article, and, finally, that a comment and cuts of all the plays produced will be printed in the next current issue of the American Review of Reviews. In addition, practically all the leading state journals carried editorial comment.

The Playmakers Association is already more than a mere campus organization; it is already an organization of the community and, it is hoped its influence will shortly be felt and recognized throughout our state, and beyond.

It seems only fair to say that the Playmakers Association promises to be one of our most distinctive campus organizations. Plans have been made and are even now being favorably considered whereby a student will be given a gold "N. C." for excellent work done in dramatics, as he is now given the pin for making an intercollege debate. In any event, the Playmakers work is here to stay. Dramatics on an intensely organized scale have come to the Hill.

In other branches the work goes on. The class in English 21, which last quarter organized into a Peace Conference, and published their own Peace Treaty and Constitution of the League of Nations,—a document that received editorial comment of a favorable nature in the New York papers, the Nation, the New Republic, the Survey, and many others, have this past quarter devoted their efforts to the production of a novel dealing with the labor problem in a typical American community. Excellent work has been done in completing two books of this three-book novel. The course has a most unique plan mapped out for the next quarter; the writing will concern the development of our Carolina state.

Writing such as this has had as appreciable effect on the student literary publications; the magazine hastily organized after Christmas is declared to be equal, if not superior, to any that has ever been produced here. The movement is progressing; the encouraging fact is that greater things shall be done.

To you who read this, whether ye be Carolina students or prospects, let it have this significance: It may not be our lot, in our lives here at Carolina, to take part in the more spectacular activities of our college life, in athletics. But if we are not naturally endowed with athletic requirements, if we may not go out on the football field and cover ourselves with mud and glory,—remember: They also serve who only sit and write.

This movement is, I think, but one part of our University's swift, new progress,—let us, all of us, attach ourselves to some activity and aid in that progress. "The old order changeth,"—we are being carried forward in the deep, strong currents of our university's progress,—our new university which will add to the glory of the past the greater glory of the future.

Let us swim with the current.

—THOMAS WOLFE.

Deferred Payment, 1919

Magazine, June 1919, 139–53

The Return of Buck Gavin: The Tragedy of a Mountain Outlaw, a folk play that Wolfe wrote for Frederick Koch's playwriting course, was well received when it was performed for local audiences in March 1919. Its success prompted Wolfe to attempt a second play, *Deferred Payment,* similar in plot to *Buck Gavin.*

In his research in the Wisdom Collection at Harvard's Houghton Library, Richard Walser discovered Wolfe's incomplete play *The Convict's Theory,* which recounts the story of a lawbreaker who returns to the mountains from the penitentiary to kill his double-crossing brother. Walser believed that it served as the genesis for *Deferred Payment,* a one-act, three-character play published in the *Magazine* (*Thomas Wolfe Undergraduate,* 94).

A.P.M.

Deferred Payment

THOMAS WOLFE

PERSONS OF THE PLAY

The Man . . . . Jack
The Woman . . . . Lucy, his wife
The Convict . . . . Jack's brother

Setting: A cabin interior. To left forefront a rude wooden table with red cloth. Thick tableware thereon. Walls garishly decorated with newspaper supplements, etc. Large stone hearth at right center. Tongs, pokers, iron kettle, and andirons. Spinning wheel. Rocker before fire. Two straight chairs at either end of table. Door at right rear. Window left rear. Exit to kitchen shed left center. Trundle bed left rear, with patchwork blanket. Lithograph over door inscribed with "God Bless Our Home!"

The Woman—worn, frail, perpetually frightened looking—is laying thick, ugly pewter stuff and iron tableware on the table. She looks toward the door

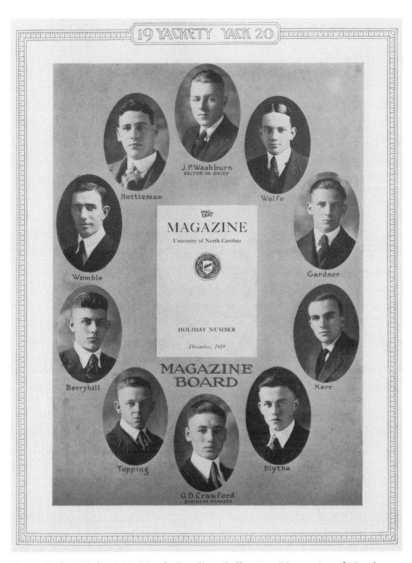

From *Yackety Yack,* 1920. North Carolina Collection, University of North Carolina at Chapel Hill

furtively, and wipes hands on a dirty apron. The sound of heavy boots outside, and an impatient rattling of door knob; then a hammering on the door.

THE WOMAN

In frightened voice

Who—who's thar?

THE MAN
Outside, in harsh voice
Lemme in, Lucy.
THE WOMAN
Wearily
Oh, hit's you. All right.
She unlocks the door. Enter the man, bestial, unshaven, gorilla-like.
THE MAN
Glowering
What th' hell's this mean? A purty welcome—th' door locked, eh? Whut fer?
THE WOMAN
I—I didn't think y'd git back so soon. Y' come earlier'n usual.
THE MAN
Well, whut uv it? Is thet any reason for keepin' th' door locked?
THE WOMAN
I—I wus afeared. I git afeared somehow, lately, when hit gits dark. I—I
didn't know when ye'd git back—ye're gone so much lately.
THE MAN
Roughly
That's nothin' t' y'—so keep yer trap closed. I'm boss uv these diggins, an' th'
sooner yer find hit out th' better fer y'.
*He scowls at her a minute, then grips her suddenly, brutally, by the wrist and
draws her to him. She shrinks back frightened.*
THE MAN
Jeeringly
My lovin' wife! Glad t' see me, ain't ye?
THE WOMAN
Oh, y've been at hit agin!
THE MAN
Mockingly
Sure. Hit's m' right.
THE WOMAN
Timidly
But—Jack—hit's not right—hit's agin th' law!
THE MAN
Thet so? Why? I use m' own cawn an' m' own still, don't I? I don't sell none
uv hit. Whut right's th' law t' stop me? I ain't ha'min' no one, an' if they come
botherin' me, by God—
He pauses ominously

THE WOMAN

No, y' don't ha'm nobody—I reckon . . . . but yerself . . . . an'—
an' me.

THE MAN

In surprise

An' ye? Gittin' all-fired high an' mighty all uv a sudden. Whut y' got t' do
with hit? I guess yer in need uv a little hoss medicine agin.

THE WOMAN

Jack—don't—be keerful! Ye hurt me last time ye—ye got this way, an' I
couldn't do m' work fer a week.

THE MAN

Sullenly

Aw, fergit it. Supper ready?

THE WOMAN

In a minute. (*He scowls.*) I—I didn't think y'd be hyeh.

THE MAN

Irritably

Fer Gawd's sake git a move on. Th' way y' moon aroun' hyeh hit's a wonder
y' git anythin' done. Now, hurry—I'm hungry. . . . . Whar's th' paper?
Come yet?

THE WOMAN

On th' table thar. I haven't opened hit yet.

THE MAN

Well, git out uv hyeh an' bring yer supper on.

*She goes out. He picks up paper and tears wrapping off, then opens it casually.
Sits down and puts boots on table, fills corncob pipe, lights it, and prepares for a
leisurely perusal of paper. He reads silently for a minute, then grows tense at something he reads, and leaps to his feet.*

THE MAN

After a minute, slowly

Gawd, he's got away—flew th' coop clean. (*He is greatly agitated, and paces
the room.*) Knocked a guard in th' head, hit says hyeh, an' made 's getaway.
I—she mustn't know uv this. (*He crumples paper in back pocket.*) Gawd!
Whut if he did come hyeh!

*He looks into fire, in great agitation. The door opens and another man comes in
quietly. He is badly dressed in ill-fitting garments, coat buttoned up tightly, hat
pulled low over his eyes; unshaven, but not bestial-looking. In fact, his features are
characterized by sensitiveness. His skin glares ghastly white under his beard. He
slowly unbuttons his coat. Under it is seen the glaring black and white shirt of
the convict.*

THE CONVICT
With soft irony
My—brother.

THE MAN
Jumping as if shot, then turning and gazing stupefied
You hyeh!

THE CONVICT
Coughing hoarsely, and grinning a ghastly grin
Glad I come, ain't y'?

THE MAN
Fiercely
Y' fool—why'd ye come hyeh? I told ye when they got ye not to try t' git away. I told y' not t' come hyeh.

THE CONVICT
Slowly
No, I reckon hit wan't th' best thing—fer ye, anyway.

THE MAN
Startled
Whut d' y' mean?

THE CONVICT
Oh—yer sech a good, law-abidin' sort uv a citizen. . . . . By th' way, how's the cawn crop this year?

THE MAN
Sullenly
Aw—ye— Look hyeh, yer a fool f'r gittin' away like this. An' hit'll go hard with ye fer gittin' th' guard. Why'd ye come hyeh?

THE CONVICT
I reckon ye know why. I told y' I'd be back.

THE MAN
If ye think I'm goin' t' hide ye, yer powerful wrong.

THE CONVICT
Quietly
I'm not askin' y' to.

THE MAN
They'll git ye mighty quick. Ye can't git away.

THE CONVICT
Coughing hollowly
I'm not tryin' to.

THE MAN

Bluntly, but a little uneasily.

Well, what d' ye come for?

THE CONVICT

Oh, ye know, even us jailbirds gits tired uv th' same ol' scenery an' all thet sort uv thing, an' we feel as if we jest has t' visit our dear friends an' relatives—sometimes. Thet's th' way I felt, anyway.

THE MAN

Sharply

Whut y' mean?

THE CONVICT

Drawling

Oh, nothin' much. . . . . I've been plannin' this hyeh leetle visit quite a bit now.

THE MAN

They'll git ye.

THE CONVICT

Thet's all right. It 'twont take me long t' make m'visit.

THE MAN

Fer Gawd's sake, whut're ye driving at?

THE CONVICT

Cain't ye guess?

The Man does not answer, but trembles. He is greatly agitated.

THE CONVICT

Continuing in slow, gentle voice

Evah see a cat play with a rat—huh?

The Man still gives no answer, but he trembles

THE CONVICT

Insistently

Did y'?

THE MAN

Yes.

THE CONVICT

Well, I'm th' cat. (*He pauses a minute.*) I reckon I've played with y' enough. Y' dirty dawg, y' know why I'm hyeh.

THE MAN

Wildly

No—no, I don't—

THE CONVICT

Shet up! I know all about that frame-up now. (*After a minute, impressively.*)
Will Carver died in th' pen two months ago.

THE MAN

Horror-struck. After a minute

Gawd! Did he—?

THE CONVICT

Grinning sardonically

Oh, don't worry ovah thet. They won't git ye. He didn't tell no one—but me.

THE MAN

But—but ye? Whut—whut y' mean?

THE CONVICT

I mean I know now who stole my gun outen my room. I mean I know who
fixed Smithers that night—with my gun—

THE MAN

Blustering

Look hyeh, d' y' mean t' accuse me—

THE CONVICT

Quietly

Quit yer bluffin'. I got th' goods on y' now. Carver, th' feller y' fixed thet deal
with, got sent up himself 'bout a year ago fer a job he did down East. Y'
never knew whut 'come uv him, eh? Well, they got 'im—not like they got
me, nobuddy *framed* him—but they got 'im clean—with th' goods.

THE MAN

Did th' damn skunk tell—tell y'—

THE CONVICT

Going on, disregarding the Man

He couldn't stand th' inside work down thar at Hell's Half-acre—*whar ye sent
me.* Hit got 'im as hit's gittin' me—hit gits lots uv us. (*He coughs hollowly.*)
Consumption—thet got 'im—but before he died, he tole me.

THE MAN

Determined to brazen it out

Well, whut uv hit now? Nobuddy knows but th' three uv us, an' he's gone.
Hit's yore word agin mine, an' ye're a jailbird. So thar y' air. Ye cain't do
nothin' 'bout hit.

THE CONVICT

Significantly

Cain't I?

THE MAN

No, y' caint.

THE CONVICT

Thet's whut y' think. But I tell y', Jack, if y'd spent th' last two months in a six-by-eight cell, a-grindin' yer teeth an' a-clawin' at yer skin, an' stuffin' yer jacket in yer mouth t' keep frum yellin', y'd be ready t' do somethin'. So I made my plan down thar in my cell. When th' cough got bad they sent me out on th' road gang. Three days ago my chance come. Hit was night. I got th' guard frum behind—I slugged him an' took 'is clo'es—an 'is gun.

THE MAN

An' here ye air?

THE CONVICT

With deadly intensity

Thar's a reason.

He moves slowly toward the man and reaches his hand into his rough convict's shirt. He pulls a blue steel automatic from his shirt. At sight of it the Man's face becomes a dirty gray.

THE CONVICT

An' now y' know why I come, I reckon.

THE MAN

Hysterically

Fer—Gawd's sake, Sam—n-not thet. I'm yer brother!

THE CONVICT

Sneering

Air ye? I fergot about thet a long time ago. Y' oughta remembered I wus yore brother.

THE MAN

Wildly

Good Gawd! Ye cain't be meanin' t'—t'— Ah—yer jokin'!

THE CONVICT

Speaking with low, intense passion

Am I? Well, hit's a rough joke on ye, Jack. I'm goin' t' kill ye.

He raises the gun slowly, its blue barrel winking ominously. The Convict seems to get a cruel satisfaction out of his sport. With a bitter smile he watches the man sink back on the table, a palsied, shaking heap.

THE MAN

Pleading

Give me a chance. I'll make hit up t' ye. I'll 'fess up. I'll take yer place in th' pen—anything—only in Gawd's name, give me a chance.

THE CONVICT

With a sneer

Ye use his name a lot, don't ye?

THE MAN
Grovelling pitiably
A chance—jest give me a chance.

THE CONVICT
Ironically
A purty chance y' gave me!

THE MAN
Eagerly
I'll fix hit up now—I'll fix hit fer ye.

THE CONVICT
Giving a croaking cough and tapping his chest, as he grins bitterly.
Ye'll fix thet, will ye? Naw, hit's too late. I'm a goner. Y've fixed me, Jack,
already—fer keeps—but I'm goin' t' fix ye 'fore I go.
*He raises the gun slowly again, and points it. The door opens, and the woman
comes in.*

THE WOMAN
Sharply
Sam. . . . . Don't!

THE CONVICT
Turning in amazement and uttering choking sob
Lucy! Here! Oh, my God!

THE WOMAN
Speaking rapidly
I stood behind th' door. I heard y'—— (*Turning fiercely to the Man who cow-
ers in the corner, she hisses:*) Y' beast—y' murderer!

THE CONVICT
Sternly
Whut 're ye doin' hyeh, Lucy?

THE WOMAN
Breaking down suddenly and sobbing
He lied t' me, Sam, he lied. He said y' wanted—wanted I sh'd—sh'd— (*She
shudders*).

THE CONVICT
Horror-struck, as it dawns on him
Air ye—his wife?
The Woman nods dumbly

THE CONVICT
In an agony of passion
God! God! God!

He is seized by a paroxysm of coughing. When he recovers, he is calm. Two hectic flushes burn in the pallor of his face. He speaks to the Man.

THE CONVICT

That's another count agin' y', Jack. I'll fix ye now.

He raises the gun

THE WOMAN

Pleading

Sam—don't—fer my sake! (*With scorn.*) Let 'im be, Sam. Don't dirty yer hands with th' likes uv him.

She grasps his arm gently and takes the revolver from him. The Man notices this with a quick, furtive glance. He sidles over to the table and grasps a long, sharp carving knife, holding it behind his back, unnoticed.

THE CONVICT

Wearily

Yeah, I reckon yer right. But y' must leave hyeh, Lucy. Now, I say. I'll go back an' give up. Don't matter much now, anyway. They won't have me much longer. (*He coughs. . . . . then continues.*) But y' go t' ol' man Judson— tell 'im I sent y'—he'll give y' work. Y' cain't stay hyeh now. Y' gotta go, Lucy. (*He pauses, then says sharply:*) D'ye heah me?

THE WOMAN

Dully

Yes, Sam.

THE CONVICT

Ye'll go?

THE WOMAN

Dully, as before

Yes, Sam.

THE MAN

Interrupting furiously

Tryin' t' separate us, huh?—lawful wedded man an' wife! Tryin' t' come 'tween us, huh? Tryin' t' threaten m' life, air ye? Well, take thet, ye meddlin' fool:

As the Convict takes a step toward the Man, the Man stabs him in the breast with the knife. The Convict reels back, staggers, and collapses in a chair. The Man gazes dully at the knife, then at the Convict, then lets the knife fall to the floor and wipes his hand furtively on his coat.

THE CONVICT

Slowly, from between white lips

You—dawg!

THE WOMAN
Horror-struck
Oh God, he's stabbed y', Sam!

THE CONVICT
Quietly
He got me.

THE WOMAN
Sobbing
Hit's my fault—I should've let ye.

THE CONVICT
Musingly, as it comes to him
No. I see it now. Y' were right. Thar's a law for sech.

THE WOMAN
A law?

THE CONVICT
Yes, an' all air bound to hit.

THE MAN
Stupefied
Gawd—what've I done?
He stares unbelievingly at the Convict, then at the knife on the floor. He gasps chokingly and looks again at the Convict, then stumbles to door.

THE MAN
With his eyes fixed on the Convict in a fascinated stare, and fumbling for the latch.
I—I cain't stay hyeh—I gotta leave hyeh.
He stumbles out blindly

THE WOMAN
Sobbing hysterically
Oh, Sam, hit's all my fault.
She clasps him almost fiercely

THE CONVICT
Smiling gently, and speaking almost inaudibly, as he strokes her hair
No, hit's all right. Hit's all right. Nothin's lost . . . . (*in a whisper*) I—love y', Lucy.

THE WOMAN
Monotonously
He got y'—I c'd've saved y'—he got y' . . . . he's gone—free!

THE CONVICT
Through stiffening lips, as he dies
No! He will pay!

A VERY SLOW CURTAIN.

"Russian Folk Song," 1919

Magazine, June 1919, 191

"Russian Folk Song" is Thomas Wolfe's earliest published piece of political satire. Wolfe's folk tragedy *Deferred Payment* was also in the June 1919 issue of the *Magazine,* but Walser in *Thomas Wolfe Undergraduate* maintained that "humor was now, no mistake about it, his intent, his sword, his strength" (80).

A.P.M.

Russian Folk Song

THOMAS CLAYTON

Whose carcass hangs from yonder tree?
His ugly face a-mocking me—
Why, that's a damnéd plutocrat
Who owns his shoes, his coat and hat,
With lots of other things—ten dollars,
A bank account, three ties and collars.

If that is so, why, he's well strung;
All such as he should be well hung.
'Tis said he did his daily work,
A deed all honest men should shirk.

'Tis said he spent his time in makin'
A home for wife; some bread and bacon
Did grace his board come every Sunday;
And he at work on time come Monday.

Ah, can it be? Then he's well dead,
As sure as I'm a Russian Red;
Such men as he, I keenly feel,
Are dangerous to the common weal.

Ah, brother, we do well in givin'
Th' rope to those who think of livin'.
Come! Let's away to Petrograd,
Where Ivan Trotzky needs us bad.

The Streets of Durham, 1919

Tar Baby, November 18, 1919, 4–5, 14

On the evening of October 18, 1919, at the Dialectic Literary Society smoker, Thomas Wolfe, who was often called upon to read and perform at these gatherings, presented three of his recent stories for the evening's entertainment. The last one, *The Streets of Durham, or Dirty Work at the Cross Roads,* is a mixture of burlesque, humorous ditties, buffoonery, and satire. His friends in the Di Society admired Wolfe for his comic gifts, and that evening's performance was a particular triumph for him.

A month later the piece was printed in the *Tar Baby,* a campus humor magazine, under its extended title *The Streets of Durham, or Dirty Work at the Cross Roads (A Tragedy in Three Muddy Acts).* For this publication, act 3 has scene 3 and scene 4 but no first and second scenes, which could have been a compositor's error or one of Wolfe's jokes (probably the latter).

The Streets of Durham was included in *A Century of College Humor,* edited by Dan Carlinsky (New York: Random House, 1971) and reprinted in 1982 as a separate publication, edited with an introduction by Richard Walser (350 copies for distribution to members of the Thomas Wolfe Society). Walser provides a description of the plot:

> With a setting of Durham's muddy streets for the play, its villain had of course to be the "scheming contractor" John Q. Asphalt. Yet a folk-play demands that common folk be in the cast; so Wolfe introduces policemen, students from Trinity College (soon to be Duke University), three Durham belles, and the *Tar Heel* editor himself. Such characters as Nemesis, History, and Father Time provide the pseudo dignity of allegory. The local elements necessary in folkplays are emphasized with references to the Malbourne Hotel, the Orpheum Theater, Bull Durham tobacco, and the city's millionaire Julian Shakespeare Carr. For a finale, as reminder that Thanksgiving was not many weeks away, Wolfe composed a paean of gratitude. . . . A delightful concoction it was! (13)

A.P.M.

The Streets of Durham

or Dirty Work at the Cross Roads
(*A Tragedy in Three Muddy Acts*)

BY TOMMY WOLFE

PERSONS OF THE PLAY

The Chorus . . . . The Durham Police Force
History . . . . Himself
Father Time . . . . Ditto
Despair . . . . The Tar Heel Editor
Nemesis . . . . A Steam Shovel with an evil eye and devouring jaws
A Scheming Contractor . . . . Mr. John Q. Asphalt

Supported by an all star cast, including shopgirls, shoplifters, mill people, ill people, butchers, bakers and candlestick makers, Trinity students dressed neatly but not gaudily in light pink shirts with green collars, together with the rest of the native population.

ACT I

SCENE I

The curtain rises on a dreary prospect. Coming faintly through the driving rain one hears the mournful whistle of the Bull Durham factory. Nemesis in the form of a steam shovel, stands by quietly with a cold sneer on his evil face. A few belated ducks swim languidly around in some of the more shallow puddles; the others are too deep. Enter two members of the Durham police force, dressed in their native regalia, and heavily armed with rubber boots. One is a sergeant, the other a plain cop. On their respective bosoms are pinned the insignia of their order, viz., namely and to-wit:

A field of green embossed and cut diagonally by a streak of yellow, the whole surmounted by two beer bottles, rampant. The orchestra plays softly the opening strains of Danny Deever.

"What are the whistles tooting for?" said Sgt. McElrade.

"Another day of Durham Bull," the new policeman said.

"What makes you look so green, so green," said Sgt. McElrade.

"I just fetched in from Appletree," the new policeman said. "For the frost was on the pumpkin and the cawn was in the bin, I hadn't had a bit of rest in Gawd alone knows when. So I joined the Durham force on Wednesday mornin'."

"What's that so pink against the sky?" said Sgt. McElrade.

"'Tis the student shirts of Trinity," the new policeman said.

"Methinks I see a tinge of green," said Sgt. McElrade.

"'Tis the collars to the shirts you've seen," the new policeman said.

"For their student body cometh in their winsome boyish way,

They're done with registration and they're marching en masse

To the Malbourne and the Orpheum and goodly cabaret

Belike you'll need your foive before the mornin'."

Enter a group of Trinity students with a gleeful shout, singing the good old business college songs.

SCENE II

College stuff: Chorus on your left, Trinity gathered around Maypole erected in center stage.

Trinity Students—

Let us gather 'round the maypole, comrades, in our happy boyish way,

Today let us be merry, tomorrow come what may.

If I should fall asleep, just wake me, wake me, brothers dear,

Tomorrow'll be the maddest, gladdest day of all the year.

For I'm to be queen of the May, brothers, I'm to be queen of the May.

(The whole chorus hits a high note as the curtain relaxes and falls.)

ACT II

SCENE I

Same as before. Enter three Durham belles whom we shall call Mary, Kate, and Minnie, mainly because those are their names.

Minnie (in consternation)—O Gawd, girls, look at the mud!

Kate—It's really quite obtuse of the authorities to permit these intolerable conditions.

Mary—I should worry; mine are silk. (They cross the street, their cheeks suffused with the delicate shy flush of maidenhood, a chorus of admiring "oh's" and "ah's" from Trinity students collected on the corner.)

Trinity student (enthusiastically)—Boni stuffi. (Latin for "good stuff.")

SCENE II

Enter Tar Heel editor, dazed. His mind is wandering. Casts wild despairing glances toward the streets.

Tar Heel Editor (laughing hysterically)—"O Fireman, save my pop-eyed child," the frantic mother cried, but the frog climbed a sycamore tree and sighed, as he sharpened his sting with a file. (From a ballad of mountain dew.)

"O mother, hear that rattling noise?" a little girl once said.

"Cheer up, my dear, 'tis your father's voice, the poor nut's brains are dead."—An old Durham folk song.)

Tar Heel Editor (regaining sanity for a moment)—O God, I would I were a duck.

ACT III

Same as before. Enter John Q. Asphalt, a scheming contractor and his co-conspirator, Nemesis, the steam shovel. Asphalt is a man with a fat hog-like face, a derby hat and prematurely grey eyes. No self-respecting playwright ever describes Nemesis.

Nemesis—When shall we two meet again. In thunder, lightning, or in rain?

Asphalt—Preferably in rain. The trouble with thunder and lightning is that their bark is usually louder than their bite. Now rain is a slow but sure assistant. Why, if it keeps on raining, I won't finish this job until the spring of 1979.

Nemesis—We'll pave this street with asphaltine and take it up again I ween, for when they find the sewers missed, they'll want 'em in real quick I wist.

Yes, if my wops will only stick fast
We'll tear them up from Hell to Breakfast.
And after that it's easy, then—
From Breakfast back to Hell again.
And if our methods cute don't fright 'em.
We'll keep 'em up ad infinitum.

Nemesis (admiringly)—You're a man after my own heart. (Arm in arm the two conspirators speak around the corner and drink to the day with a bottle of Bevo, pilfered from Gen. Julian S. Carr's cellar.)

SCENE III

Enter chorus of natives singing the native song of lamentation. Chorus:

> We never get to see the neighbors,
> Since they ripped up all our streets, bejabbers.
> And it's us that's telling yo' we're sorry,
> That we let them fix our streets, begorry.
> We sure did pull a big fat bone
> When we let 'em do it, ohchone, ohchone!

(In the distance can be heard the hoarse, grating chuckle of Nemesis, followed by the high falsetto cackle of Asphalt.) The natives shiver and look at each other muttering: "I reckon we had better be getting along home, there's dirty work ahead."

SCENE IV

Forty-seven years have elapsed. During this time the audience gets tired of waiting and goes out. The curtain rises on the same street as in Act I. It is still raining. Nemesis, the steam shovel, has moved two blocks down the street. History and Father Time make their first appearance; they come in together and converse.

Father Time—I'm gittin' tired of waitin'.

History—It took me twenty-seven years to write a history of the war.

> To count the graves, the tombs and biers,
> Also the near beers—but I'll swear
> In thirty-seven different lingos
> There Durham streets have all the jingoes
> Beat that ever jingoed. Now my song
> Is something like this, "Oh, Lord, how long!"

Father Time (fiercely)—I'm an old man an' I deserve some consideration. It's all the fault of that young scoundrel there (he shakes his fist at Nemesis whose back is turned).

History—Let's fix him.

Time—Done. (He pulls his trusty Smith & Wesson from his pocket. His gun coughs and spits fire. Nemesis falls, mortally wounded, shot through his waistcoat and with his suspenders cut to ribbons. With a joyous shout the chorus of natives [including students and police force] rush out on stage uttering noises of delirious delight.)

First Native (hoarsely)—At last! At last! We are saved. Drink! Drink! Strong drink! (The popping of corks may be heard and we gaze upon a wild debauch of intoxication as the natives reel from the effects of eleven bottles each of Pepsi-Cola. They continue their wild orgy of joy, putting pennies recklessly in chewing gum slots and laughing insanely as they stagger around. Finally two or three of the more sane ones come forward and sing the native song of Thanksgiving.)

Chorus—From the muddy lands with which our feet were shackled,

To this freedom, with hope's brightest lamp imbued,

Is the farthest cry that ever roared or cackled,

Or one might say, farthest cry that ever crewed.

> Come let us hence
> To some point thence

To celebrate the death of dull Misgiving,

To crown our joy with feats of great Thanksgiving;

Yea, since the corkscrew's lost its pull

Let's open up a can of Bull.

> (The natives scream with delight. They are still screaming as)

THE CURTAIN FALLS

The Crisis in Industry, 1919

(Chapel Hill: University of North Carolina Department of Philosophy, 1919)

At the June 1919 commencement ceremonies it was announced that Thomas Wolfe was awarded the Worth Prize in Philosophy for the best thesis, *The Crisis in Industry*, submitted in Professor Horace Williams's class. Williams was reported to have stated that the prize was awarded to the most brilliant student he ever had and that the recipient would earn a place of distinction in the life of the university.

In the essay Wolfe champions the cause of labor against industry and argues that capital must recognize labor's right to self-determination and must assist in the creation of an "individual democracy,—a system of democratic co-operation in industry with equal rights and responsibilities for labor and capital." Wolfe thought of himself as part of the working class. His father was a stonecutter, and his mother ran a boardinghouse.

The Crisis in Industry, Wolfe's first separate publication, was published, with a brief introduction by Horace H. Williams, by the University of North Carolina Philosophy Department in an edition of two hundred copies. The fourteen-page pamphlet is one of the most sought-after of Wolfe rarities; fewer than a dozen copies are known to exist.

In *The Window of Memory: The Literary Career of Thomas Wolfe* (Chapel Hill: University of North Carolina Press, 1962), Richard S. Kennedy judged that of all Wolfe wrote during his undergraduate years at Chapel Hill, only *The Crisis in Industry* showed a "glimmer of the force that was to come" and "gave a hint of the creative turbulence that was latent in him" (54).

Nearly sixty years after its original appearance, two facsimile editions were published: one by Palaemon Press (Winston-Salem, N.C., 1978) in two hundred copies and another by Ballinger's Used and Rare Books (Hillsborough, N.C., 1978) in three hundred copies, fifty of which were distributed in a cardboard folder with copies of Richard Walser's *Prologomena to Thomas Wolfe's "A Crisis in Industry."* Numbers 51–300 were distributed with an inserted reduced facsimile of the *Prologomena*.

A.P.M.

UNIVERSITY OF NORTH CAROLINA
DEPARTMENT OF PHILOSOPHY

THE CRISIS IN INDUSTRY

(CROWNED WITH THE WORTH PRIZE)

_____

THOMAS WOLFE

_____

CHAPEL HILL
PUBLISHED BY THE UNIVERSITY
1919

This publication qualifies as Wolfe's first book. North Carolina Collection, University of North Carolina at Chapel Hill

Introduction

The Worth Prize is maintained by Mr. C. W. Worth, '82, in memory of his father, Mr. D. G. Worth, Wilmington, N. C. The prize was established in 1882 by Mr. D. G. Worth in appreciation of the excellent work done in Philosophy by Mr. C. W. Worth. The list of Worth Prize men, headed by Mr. C. W. Worth, is a unique group. Some of them have now national reputations. One has published more books than any other alumnus of the University. One of these books, The Philosophy of Education, has been translated into four languages, including that of Japan.

The prize is awarded to the best thesis submitted in the courses in Philosophy and consists in having this thesis printed. To achieve this honor gives a man distinction in University life.

When one thinks of the subjects studied in these theses, he marvels at the courage of the men. They enjoy full freedom in this matter and reach their own conclusions. The instructor seeks to give vital stimulus and then submerge.

Mr. Thomas Wolfe, the winner of the prize for 1919, makes an innovation, as to subject. He tells us about Industry.

The students who look below the surface will agree that Industry is now the source of human anxiety. Many believe we are face to face with one of those profound storms that come in man's life every few centuries.

So far man has been unable to pass through such an upheaval without the liberal use of big violence. The result has been vast loss and deep suffering. Not only the body, but the mind and soul have suffered. It may be that violence is an instrument of progress.

If Philosophy shall be able to throw any light upon the problem of Industry, or aid in advancing gentler methods of progress, the effort justifies itself.

H. H. WILLIAMS.

Chapel Hill, N. C., 1919.

The Crisis in Industry

"Wars," the philosopher says, "are the birth pangs of truths." "Great wars," he continues, "are the birth pangs of master truths." We have just seen a great war come to its close.

If any truth has come from that war, it is the truth of modern labor becoming conscious of itself as a vital, breathing, compelling force. The industrial problem looms before us in an almost menacing aspect. We know today that the issue demands immediate settlement. Victorious in our war with the common foe we are today appalled by the mutterings of something far more dreadful,—industrial civil strife. Let us consider, for a minute, the viewpoint of the detached observer. One of Japan's most distinguished statesmen, Count Okuma, looking across the world at the great war just closed, declared it to be nothing less than the death of modern civilization. Just as the civilizations of Babylon, Egypt, Greece, Carthage, and the Roman Empire have crumbled in succession, so, in his opinion, our modern civilization is even now going the same way. Whether this be true or not, it is certain that from the world struggle we may see the destruction of an industrial civilization which the workers will not want to build back. And the danger now is that at this period of crisis, it may be easier to pass into ruin than to move onward. There is the problem.

In the midst of all these volcanic outbreaks of industrial trouble in the different parts of our country, thinking people are asking each other, "What does labor want?" It is a puzzling question. The wages for which labor works are higher than ever before, the living and working conditions of the workers are almost ideal compared with those of even a generation ago,—the whole industrial scheme seems regulated on a more humane scale.

But it becomes evident, at this time, that these petty, paltry bickerings, for a six-hour day, higher wages, meal times, and all the rest, do not in even the slightest degree represent the fundamental nature of these men's demands, —demands that became clearly defined during the war, and that now cry for answer.

On the other hand, I do not assume for a minute that the doctrines of Socialism or Bolshevism demanding the destruction of the capitalist system and advocating the conscious class warfare represents the attitude of labor in general, or that such methods as these are the motivating purposes of any large group of leaders and workers with the exception, perhaps, of one or two restricted areas.

No—the labor movement has nothing in common with this kind of doctrine. I believe it realizes the fundamental right of capital to a share in the business of production; what it protests against is the fact that under the present system, labor itself does not have a share, and it asserts that its right to an equal share is just as true, and just as fundamental as the right of capital.

The fact that the great body of workers have not defined sharply the nature of their demands does not, for a minute, indicate that they do not know what they want. The awakening of labor may not as yet be complete; its consciousness of itself may not be realized to the utmost. I do not think it is yet, but its newly gained knowledge is not obscure. The whole experience of the war has been to clarify its vision.

Labor today is in active revolt against the whole system whereby its labor, the product of its blood, bone, sinew, and brain is treated as a commodity— something to be bought at will, the price of which may be forced up or down, just as the price of flour or sugar. If labor is a commodity, then its demands that it have a directive power in the expenditure of its own labor, its assumption that it is engaged in a business with capital and that business is production, its statement that its contribution to that business is just as essential as the contribution of capital, and that, therefore, it should be entitled to the control of this business with capital on a basis of equal co-partnership,—if, I say, the assumption that labor is a commodity is correct, then labor is unjustified in these beliefs and demands. For a commodity, to my mind, is devoid of life, or, if it possesses life, that life is insensate and devoid of consciousness.

But I do not believe that labor is a commodity. Labor has life—in fact, labor is life. Remove life and there is no labor. No one would say that a machine labors;—it runs. The desire to work, to labor, is fundamental in a man, it is not a mechanical process; it comes from his inmost being, I sincerely believe.

There is a sacredness about labor, it is of a religious nature even—and religion is fundamental in the lives of men.

If, then, labor is life, and not insensate; if labor is possessed of an intelligent consciousness of itself and the workings of its life, it becomes manifest that labor itself, in the intelligent consciousness of itself, becomes its own unit of value, the directive force of its own working, the source of its own purposes and that, in short, it dominates its own existence, and cannot, by right, be forced to the obedience of any outward imposition.

What labor wants, as I see it, is its right to self-direction. Capital does not recognize this right. Whereas the swift, sure progress of labor consciousness is today well marked and may be, at all times, clearly defined, I am unable to discover a corresponding process on the part of capital. These capitalist folk, your owning and directing, and managing people, remain blind to the fundamentals of the problem. In a few isolated places, one perhaps catches a gleam, but, for the rest, they cannot understand the attitude of labor. The trouble is: Capital is now as static as it was fifty years ago. As some one has said, the chief difference is golf.

These men, for the most part, seem to have learned neither humanity or caution from the tedious times our nation has gone through. Instead of awakening to the new sense of values, they rather brand, as does a large part of society, the workers as "I. W. W.'s," "Slackers," "Bolshevists,"—workers who, becoming conscious of their social and human value, realizing their problem is a human one, are striving to carry that new sense into a reformed industrial system.

The capitalist class do not seem to realize that the "old order changeth," that it is changed, God willing, for all time. The significance of the war seems lost on them. But—there can be no patchwork reconstruction now. I do not believe that now that the war is over, now that we have emerged from the holocaust, that what remains to be reconstructed is this or that bureau of government, this or that machine of administration. No—the meaning of the war is more fundamental, more vital than any of these. The whole society must be reconstructed. Labor sees this, in general capital does not.

Thus, as we have seen, the labor group is in active revolt against the old system. They know it must change. And they are trying to change it now, using as their method the so-called "direct action," the strike.

But—here another problem arises. It is plain labor sees the problem, manifestly they are clear in their knowledge of what they want,—but, do they see the solution? Is force a remedy of the vast industrial problem?

The unrestricted use of force by both classes, capitalist and labor, is, I think, a dangerous sequence, the terrible reflex action of the giant strife that has been waged throughout the world. It manifests itself now in class warfare here. Inflamed by privations and suffering, it shows itself as civil war in Russia and Germany.

The war parallel, I think, is a good one. The neutral observer, which, in the industrial strife, is supposedly the citizenship without the two classes, may protest against the quality of a justice, which, acting from itself, is the judge of its own cause, and the vindication of itself through its triumphant force. It is the age-old idea of "Might Is Right." But might is not right, and can never vindicate its cause. Force everywhere sweeps aside its moral obligations and runs its own course unmindful of the rights of others. Insistent on its own rights, it forgets that words "right" and "duty" are, or should be, inseparably linked. What of the duty to the neutral, if I may use the war parallel again? If two boys fight in the street a crowd gathers to watch them,—they are separated,—the crowd goes its way. In a class warfare waged between labor and capital, the crowd, which is the third group, the consumers of production, cannot look on with the detached viewpoint. No! The problem is so vast, it is so close to the heart of national life, that the whole body of the nation is affected deeply, powerfully. The question yet remains to be answered: Can any class, insistent on its own rights, obtain them with rampant force, at the expense of universal suffering?

This idea of force used in the interests of the class is the natural builder of its own rights, the satisfaction of its in-wrought cravings is expressed unconsciously, but masterfully, in the exclamation of the Frenchman, Pichon: "Has the victor no rights over the vanquished?"

I will answer the Frenchman that the victors have no rights over the vanquished because of their victory. I do not believe the use of force ever settled any problem. Class warfare is being waged throughout the country now. The strike—the direct action, the method of force is the common agency. Whenever the labor group obtains its demands or part of them, a shout of triumph goes up from labor's ranks. Similarly, when capital is successful in hold-out methods, there is great rejoicing among capitalists. The victory of the moment has been won; these men do not pause to consider the fact that they are as far away from a solution, nay, further, than ever. When we consider this question reasonably, when we consider the fundamental demand of labor that it engage in business with capital on a basis of mutual responsibility, and mutual democratic co-partnership, a demand admitted in isolated cases by capital,—we see plainly that instead of being drawn closer together until they meet at a solution, the method of force has only served to antagonize the two classes, until now they face each other in separate armed camps, ready, at the provocation of prejudice, to wage blind, futile warfare.

The solution to the problem is, I think, fairly obvious. Intelligent people today admit, nor can any decent-minded person deny, in this day, that the demand of labor for democratic co-operation is unreasonable. Indeed, in a political democracy, the only natural parallel here would be industrial democracy. We feel today that capitalist absolutism must go, that any form of capitalist domination is hateful. Likewise, we know that a reversal of the system whereby labor would hold the dominant position would be just as undesirable.

There is, to my mind, but one adequate solution. That solution, broadly put, is industrial democracy,—a system of democratic co-operation in industry with equal rights and responsibilities for labor and capital.

It is significant to note that the first two methods depend on force for their maintenance—the last method depends on co-operation,—on the inherent willingness of men to listen to reason. Is there not a living hope for us that the principles of democracy and self-determination, which are being put to the test today in government, can meet the test in industry? It seems to me that there is a compelling parallelism here, that the success or failure in the one phase stands for a corresponding success or failure in the other.

It is too much, to my mind, to hope that the labor class will effect this desirable solution by themselves. They see, as we know, the problem, they have come into a realization of their right, but they do not see a proper solution.

The method of force is, I believe, a natural, but a distinctly menacing sequence to the war just ended.

If, in the fact of labor's display of force, government misunderstands it, and retaliates with a rival and superior display of force, then let us say farewell to our hopes of democracy. Capital could, I suppose, conscript an army large enough to quell for the time rebellious labor. But, even if the strife which sets brother against brother should succeed, labor would still be alive in the flaming spirit of revolt.

We cannot consider labor a category; it is human—a mass of men and women workers. We may stigmatize the labor movement all we choose,—we may call it selfish, menacing, rebellious, thoughtless—any of these names, but the fact remains that labor has possession of a great truth.

Labor knows that the system—the blind system that treats man as an adjunct to the machine, has nearly crushed out the little lives of the workers. And it is making its effort to get this blind power in hand.

As I have said, I do not think labor has attained a full consciousness of itself; that will evolve. I think some phases of the movement are faulty.

Labor makes its mistake, I think, in making the same demands for the mass of the workers.

In this respect, it seems to be a mass movement. But it is evident that the capabilities of individual workmen must always be considered. The capacity of one individual for work may be either greater or less than those of another. Such a thing as real equality in this respect is, to my mind, hardly possible.

It is granted, perhaps, that individuals have equal opportunities for work under a reformed industrial system. It does not hold, however, that individuals have equal capacities for work, and labor today in its onward movement has manifestly not taken this into consideration.

This, however, is a natural mistake and one which may be remedied.

And now, how does the problem stand?

We see labor has come into a realization of its self as a body vital with the power of life, intelligent as to its workings, and sure of its function in industry. We realize that no reasonable solution to our problem will ever be obtained by the use of force—by the strike which breaks out sporadically at this time in various parts of the country. The solution to labor appears to be the strike, the use of force. That is no true solution.

Now, since this problem is one that affects the vitals of national life and unity, it is obviously the business of government to aid the workers to attain the true solution.

If the government sees only on the surface, and attempts to crush labor by a superior display of force, the result will be nothing less than terrible civil strife.

As it seems to me, the issue stands squarely before the government. Labor no longer has faith in government as a legislative remedy for their problem. Labor puts no dependence in the ballot today—this means is inadequate,—we have in its place the strike, the direct action.

Where lies the fault? Largely, I think, with government. A few months ago one of the most memorable sessions of Congress in the nation's history came to a close. It was memorable not for what it had done but for what it had left undone. The industrial condition during the months immediately following the signing of the armistice grew and is growing, as I write this, continually more menacing. Congress, with great care, kept away from the industrial problem. The session, for the most part, was concerned by petty, party bickerings, back-bitings and partisan politics of a paltry nature. I say this with no attempt to be sensational, with no spirit of bitterness,—it seems an obvious statement of fact.

Faced with a condition like this, what can labor do? The final solution is left for government. In the first place, what is our conception of democracy? Some say it is the rule of the majority. If this is so, what chance have the minority for the attainment of their honest desires?

Is this a true conception of democracy? It is, perhaps, the accepted conception, but is this not a sordid, insensate thing? We think of democracy as alive, as vital.

Can the majority establish its cause by mere right of numbers? I do not think so. The right of numbers is analogous to the right of force. As well might we say the gladiator should die because the majority of the Roman populace turned down its thumbs.

Yet, here is a living obstacle. With the powerful press of the country denouncing labor as insurrectionary and menacing, with public opinion being moulded adversely day by day, with the denunciation of the whole capitalist system, what can a minority group do? Labor is employing the organized community threat—the strike, to get its demands.

What must the government do? If the majority turn down the thumbs to a minority group,—that group is subjected to a democratic tyranny,—contradictory as the statement may sound.

Likewise, the minority may retaliate by the strike method and the business of the whole community will be paralyzed. It is a reversible action.

This condition must be changed. The real problem, most evidently, is not arriving at the solution, which, expressed broadly, is industrial democracy. The solution is evident. The problem now is making the solution possible for the labor group. This must be done by the government.

The only possible way this can be done, as I see it, is to allow labor itself to determine its inner workings. It amounts to an industrial application of "self-determination."

The prejudice of the many can no longer, in justice, be allowed to curtail the conscious development of the few; the workers owe a duty of production to the nation,—this, they must fulfill,—as for the industrial status they desire, this must be established and maintained by co-operative means between and by the two groups of industry.

It is the right of these men to their own conscious development,—it is something they must decide within themselves without any outward imposition.

The principle of self-determination, intended primarily for the small nation, which our democracy now advocates, must finally, I think, be used industrially, as well as politically. And—government must recognize and promote this.

With a feeling almost of regret I come to my conclusion.

The problem that once to me was economic is now plainly and undeniably human. It deals with the lives of men and women, their right to the conscious development of their selves.

What I have written gives me no satisfaction. For the mutterings of a coming strike become daily more threatening. Force, the blind weapon, is being used extensively,—may I not say exclusively?

What will the future bring? I do not know. Is the statement of the Japanese to come true? Are we facing the destruction of our modern civilization? Again, I do not know.

Will the blood of our young men be expended—this time in civil strife,—family against family, brother against brother? God forbid!

Concerning Honest Bob, 1920

Magazine, May 1920, 251–61

When the gubernatorial campaign heated up in the late winter of 1920, Thomas Wolfe became interested in politics but vehemently disapproved of the empty rhetoric of most of the candidates. He has been credited with the editorial titled "Useful Advice to Candidates," which appeared in the February 28, 1920, issue of the *Tar Heel* (see "Attributions").

In his *Thomas Wolfe Undergraduate,* Richard Walser claims that once the state gubernatorial campaign was out of the way, Wolfe turned his attention to campus politics: "He deplored 'political rings' and 'confidential talks,' 'personal attacks,' and dormitory canvassing at night. He had only scorn for the hypocrisy of men running for office who considered it brazen and unbecoming to say so. Two or more campus political organizations were needed, with candidates and their supporters announcing platforms and conducting campaigns 'in an open manner.' His editorial temper was reflected in 'Concerning Honest Bob,' the last play he wrote at Chapel Hill" (115).

A.P.M.

Concerning Honest Bob

T. C. WOLFE

PERSONS OF THE PLAY

A Sophomore . . . . .Mr. Alf Cocksure
A Graduate . . . . .Mr. Boise Useddit
A Senior . . . . .Mr. Edward Wiseman
A Junior . . . . .Mr. Robert Goodman
    (Known to his admirers as "Honest Bob, the students' friend.")

(*The curtain rises on the living-room of one of our sumptuous two-room suites. The walls are garishly decorated with many colored pennants—showing a good eye for color but a bad one for selection. Elon, Guilford, and dear old Wake Forest are represented, to say nothing of one done in tinsel and gold of "Asheville—The Land of the Sky." Various rollicking college scenes of the vintage of 1892 are also here—a group of merry college youths with foaming steins, a bit of gentle horseplay with the Freshman (they are painting the college colors on him) and finally a thrilling football landscape with the pigskin hero wearing shin and nose guards. Clippings from "The Cosmopolitan," "The Police Gazette" and "The Theater" give a modern touch to the room. Under a green lamp shade and on a pine table a Sophomore is writing—not a theme, we dare not accuse him—but to his latest amour. His reference book is a folded piece of pink paper, which he consults frequently. The Sophomore is the only dignified character in this play. A Senior and a graduate come in now and the Senior, contrary to all precept, does not look particularly dignified. His air is rather that of the blasé man of the world, or better still, the air of one who has lived and suffered; a man who knows the vicissitudes of life and yet is determined to bear himself bravely through this vale of tears. The graduate is young at the business of being a graduate and his forced air of sophistication is rather pitiful. He is not a success.)*

The Senior. Hello—Alf.

The Soph. Come in, boys.

(*They come in and sit down.*)

The Senior. Who're you writing?

The Soph (*with great enthusiasm*). The finest girl in—

The Senior (*cynically*). Who is she this time?

The Soph (*turning a brick red*). I'm with this girl to stay—why, listen to this letter—(*He reads*): "And Alf, dearest boy, I think of you constantly day and night and wonder what you are doing. Dear boy, you don't know what high ambitions I have for you——"

The Graduate (*interrupting with some wise sophistry*). My dear fellow, the height of a girl's ambition is about six feet—

The Sophomore (*furiously*). Is that so?—You clever devil, where'd you read that—in *Snappy Stories*?

(The GRAD. *smiles tolerantly at him.* The SENIOR *shakes his head cynically at* The GRAD.)

The Senior. What fools these Sophomores be!

The Soph (*nervously—forgetting all the laws of hospitality*). And what damn idiots these Seniors and Graduates be—Yah!

The Senior (*soothingly*). To be sure, my boy, to be sure—Now go on and write your little letter.

(*But* The SOPH *turns half away from the table and his visitors and sulks.*)

The Senior (*after a moment*). Where's Honest Bob—the student's friend?

The Soph. Politicing, I guess—You know spring elections come next week.

The Graduate. You know, your undergraduate activities amuse me—campus politics—ha, ha!—it's positively funny.

The Soph (with irony). Go on and laugh—this is a place of amusement—Amuse you—ha, ha!—I bet it was a serious enough business to you last year.

The Senior (quickly). Not last year, Alf—you don't mean that. You know we Seniors never dabble in politics.

The Soph. All right, my lily-white friend—when you were a Junior—then.

The Senior (laughs slyly). That's the year, you remember, you posed as the students' friend.

The Graduate. That's been two years ago—you have no right to bring it up on me now—I was a mere boy.

The Senior (musingly). This bug of politics is a funny proposition. It usually stings a Sophomore—in the spring a Sophomore's fancy lightly turns to thoughts of politics—witness our young friend over here who is a horrible example of what I mean.

The Sophomore (angrily). Here, now, this is carrying a good thing too—

The Senior (not noticing the interruption). The work of the Sophomore politician is crude at all times—it has not attained the finish and smoothness of our Junior friend; the Sophomore laughs loudly at all his friends' jokes and he slaps them on the back with a patronizing, "Pretty good, old boy, pretty good!" It is the Sophomore who enters the classroom five minutes late that all may look and behold, the Sophomore who—

The Soph. Look here—I don't do any of those things.

The Senior (soothingly). No, of course not, my young friend. You are the one outstanding exception.

The Soph (bitterly). Your young friend! How old do they grow 'em where you come from? But (with irony) rave on, Philosopher!

The Senior. But the Junior—Ah! there you have the graduate politician. He works in a quiet, unobtrusive way, and his virtues are extolled by his friends. He knows that it is best that his friends do the work—he sees the need of organization; thus we have the first organization, known on the campus as the "Ring." The "Ring" works through the class quietly but surely, holding their candidate in the background. In an atmosphere of mystery he shows up to best advantage.

The Graduate (thoughtfully). Yes, that's true; you're right there.

The Senior (significantly). Of course, you ought to know—But to proceed: The Junior politician is a character of nobility; he is prompted always (it becomes known) by love for the "dear old University," and by his continual efforts "for the good of the Class"—as an example of what I mean (*The door opens here and Bob Goodman, the Junior, comes into the room*). Why, here he is now—Honest Bob, the students' friend—an example than which, I must say, there is none than whicher.

Goodman (*sullenly*). At it again, I see. Can't you ever stay off of me with this stuff about my "politicing"? That's something I've never done—

The Senior (*smiling*). They all say that—and what's more, they all believe it—

Goodman (*in disgust*). Aw, Hell! what's the use of trying to tell anything to a bunch like this! (*To* THE GRADUATE) Are you coming to the meeting of Sigma Omega tonight?

The Graduate. No, of course not. We graduates are not interested in undergraduate organizations, you know.

The Junior (*with elaborate politeness*). Oh, yes, to be sure, of course, I crave your pardon. I forgot you were no longer a boy like the rest of us— now that you have become a man, you have put away childish things—I understand; pardon me for suggesting it!

The Graduate. You know, your sarcasm doesn't affect me—I don't care for the opinion of other people any way—what they think of me makes no difference to me.

The Junior (*with an evil glitter in his eye*). Oh, is that so?—Well, I always have thought you a damn fool.

(*A look of positive pain comes over* THE GRADUATE's *face, mingled somewhat with astonishment.*) What—you call *me* a fool—*me!*

The Junior (*calmly*). Yes, you—you're the man I mean—I am pointing my finger right at you.

Grad (*hotly*). Fool yourself—that's what you are. (*Passionately, as he warms to his subject*) I leave it to the crowd here if I'm any bigger fool than you are—Why, I'll argue it out with you here and now and prove that you're a bigger fool than I am. (*He is quite eloquent by now.*)

The Junior (*with quiet triumph*). Behold, gentlemen, the man who doesn't care for the opinion of others—look at him now—and a pretty sight he is.

(THE GRADUATE *gets up, grabs his hat and angrily goes out of the room.*)

The Senior. You've got his goat now.

The Junior. He'll recover. I've seen him like this before. Alf (*to* SOPH), I'm going to shave, are your tools in the next room?

Alf. Yeh—go to it. Have you been to the Gym yet?

The Junior (*as a train of gloomy thoughts are started*). Yeh. I just came.

Alf. How are the showers?

The Junior (*bitterly*). Shower, Alf—not *showers.* This is a singular shower, a very singular shower. It has remained faithful to the student body all through its long life and now in its ripe old age some brutal master still works it overtime. Just think, Alf, what a tragedy it is—that poor old shower working that way in its declining old age. It makes me weep.

The Soph (*getting up*). Come on, Senior, let's go get the mail. There's nothing else to do. So long, Bob. (*They go out.*)

(THE JUNIOR *goes into the next room and emerges presently, coatless and collarless, with a shaving stick and a brush in his hand. He lathers his face. He goes back into the second room swinging the door behind him. Steps are heard outside. Enter two classmates—typical campaign managers now (we have them yearly) looking for a dark horse in the morrow's campaign.*)

The First. No one in, thank heaven. Now let's talk this thing over, Jim. We'll run either Bob Goodman or Johnson, that's agreed, and of the two—

The Second (*with some heat*). I'm in favor of Johnson; Bob Goodman's always impressed me as being too slick a politician.

The First. I don't agree with you. He speaks to 'em all; but he doesn't boot any of 'em—You know, it's no crime to treat people decent.

The Second (*sneers*). Yeh!—and the way he does it it's mighty good politics.

The First. You're wrong—Bob hasn't got a politicking bone in him—I know that fellow—why, he wouldn't run for any job on the campus, if he knew a ring was working for him.

The Second (*with conviction*). I'll betcha on it. He'd jump at the chance in a minute if he could.

The First. Listen—I'll show you. We'll put up that kind of a proposition to him. Tell him we can get him elected with the aid of a little organization canvassing the dorms. Do you see?

The Second. Well, he's going to refuse—I'm sure of that, and if he does—

The Second. I'll beg his pardon and be strong for him for anything up to President of the United States—But if he doesn't refuse—

The First. No chance—but if he doesn't refuse we'll brand him as a politician and drop him.

The Second. Good enough. Now let's find him and put it up to him.

The First. Let's look down stairs—if he's not there we'll come back and wait for him. He'll be back soon, any way.

(*They go out. The back door slowly opens and* THE JUNIOR, *after peering in, comes softly out, tiptoeing. He has forgotten that his face is covered with lather and that he holds his shaving brush in one hand. He is exultant.*)

The Junior (*exultantly, tiptoeing across the room*). Aha! aha! So that's their game. (*After a moment, piously*) O why is Heaven so good to me?

(*Downstairs the opening and slamming of doors may be heard and the shouted inquiries, "Is Bob Goodman in here?" and the shouted answers, "No," "Haven't seen him tonight."*)

Goodman (*meditating quickly*). Now if I can get out of the room and across the hall into Blakely's room without making any noise everything will

Wolfe (back row, center) with other members of the Pi Kappa Phi fraternity at the University of North Carolina, 1919–20. From *Yackety Yack,* 1920. North Carolina Collection, University of North Carolina at Chapel Hill

be tanlac—(*But even as he is talking he goes into the next room, gets on his coat, wipes off the lather, and comes out again hastily tieing his tie. He goes softly to the door, looks out, and steps out, closing the door gently. Across the hall another door may be heard to softly open and close and in a minute the heavy clatter of the two Juniors coming up the stairs is again heard. They burst into the room somewhat breathless from their exertions.*)

The First. Well, he's bound to come in soon, any way (*consulting his watch*). It's ten-thirty now.

The Second. Now look here, Ed, don't you let the cat out of the bag—do you hear—

The First (*irritably*). Let the cat out of the bag? What do you mean?

The Second. Don't fail to be serious. Don't let this bird Goodman know this is a frame-up. Why (*he reddens at the thought*) if he is straight I'm in a hell of a fix anyhow—I owe him a flat apology, that's all.

The First (*confidently*). Well, you'd better be getting your little speech ready—I *know* this boy.

(*The sound of some one coming up the stairs is heard. They look at each other expectantly. Goodman enters the room. He is quite cool and possessed now and shows no signs of his recent perturbation.*)

Goodman (*pleasantly*). Good evening, gentlemen. (*They nod.*)

The First. Hello, Bob, where've you been all night?

Goodman (*lying with an ease born of long practice*). At the library, working up a thesis—why, have you been looking for me?

The First (*confidentially*). Yes, Bob, sit down. We want to talk to you about the election to-morrow. (*Still more confidentially*) Say, who do you think is a good man for the Class presidency?

Goodman (*apparently somewhat embarrassed*). Why,—I don't know, Ed. You know I've been busy this spring, and I haven't paid much attention to politics—it never did interest me much. (*He says this with a laugh.*)

The First Junior. Listen, Bob, Jim over here and I have been talking this thing over and we've about concluded that you're the logical man for the place.

Goodman (*in the greatest astonishment*). Me—do you mean me? (*They both nod.*)

The First. Yes, you—Bob. Now here's our scheme: You've got friends enough to pull you through but we've got to have some organization behind you to get 'em together before the election. Now Jim and I will canvass the Class to-morrow—if you'll agree to run—and get everything sewed up for you—after that it'll be easy.

Goodman (*in slow astonishment that there can be so much wickedness among mankind*). Do you mean that you will ask my classmates to vote for me?

The First Junior. Sure.

Goodman (*springing to his feet furiously and pounding the table viciously*). Do you realize what you are asking me to do—me—me? (*He pounds his chest for dramatic effect.*) After living on this campus for three years without a blot on my name—you come to me with this sort of proposal—Gawd, gentlemen, it makes me see red!

The Second Junior (*soothingly*). Now, now, Goodman, we meant no harm—let me explain.

Goodman (*sorrowfully now*). Explain! There can be no explanations—only intense regret for me that I should live to see two of my classmates disgrace themselves and insult me—Gawd knows, I have my faults, but I have never stooped to politics. (*He is overcome here and bows his head.*)

The First Junior (*pacifically*). Wait a minute, Bob, before you cuss us out. This was all a frame-up. We wanted to see if you would fall for this kind of a proposition. You have done just what I thought you would. We framed up on you not ten minutes ago in this very room. Now we want to run you any way. We'll run you straight and advertise this event; we can get you elected all right.

The Second Junior. Just another thing, Goodman. I want to apologize for doubting you. I proposed the frame-up—but now I see my mistake and I'll back you to the limit.

Goodman (*with touching nobility*). Ah! my friends, the nomination means little to me now, the main fact is that you have vindicated yourselves in my opinion.

(*The two look at him in open awe. They realize they are beholding one of nature's noblemen. Goodman's difficulties seem to be over now, but just at this minute* THE SOPH *returns alone from the P. O.*)

The Soph. No mail for you, Bob; did you finish shaving? (*Goodman frowns at him, but* THE SOPH *sees the two visitors*). Oh, hello, boys—we'll have a real political convention when you two and Honest Bob get together. (*Goodman looks murderously at him.*)

The F. J. (*laughing*). We two, perhaps—but leave Bob out of it. We framed up on him in here while ago, offered to campaign for him, and he not only refused when he came in, but cussed us out to boot—

The Soph. When he came—Say (*to Goodman*), where've you been?

Goodman (*regaining his composure*). Up at the library.

The Soph (*beginning to see daylight*). How long?

Goodman (*with perfect composure and not even choking*). Since supper. (*Even* THE SOPH *is jarred at this.*)

The Soph (*beginning to laugh*). No—you can't bribe Honest Bob, gentlemen—it can't be done.

The F. J. Good night, Bob—we'll have to be going now. We'll see you tomorrow.

Goodman (*gravely*). Good night, gentlemen.

(*They go out.*)

Goodman (*viciously*). You idiot! Every time you open your mouth you try to cut not only your own throat but mine, too.

The Soph (*gasping for breath*). Honest Bob—the People's Friend—refusing their vile offer—and he heard it all! Oh, but you're a hellion—

Goodman (*grinning sheepishly*). Nothing else to be done. I was penned up in the back room—I couldn't help it, you know.

The Soph. What a nerve! Say, you don't need any Tanlac.

Goodman. Yes, and you're mighty lucky not to be needing a coffin. I thought the jig was up when you came in—If you ever tell (*he pauses ominously*).

The Soph. What?

Goodman. They'll have to gather your scattered remains and carry them off in a basket. Let's go to bed.

THE CURTAIN

"1920 Says a Few Words to Carolina," 1920

In *Yackety Yack '20* (Chapel Hill: University of North Carolina, 1920), 51

In the 1920 *Yackety Yack* classbook, the list of Thomas Wolfe's undergraduate activities and honors exceeded that for any other student in the year's graduating class. Below his photograph Wolfe was described as one who could "do more between 8:25 and 8:30 than the rest of us can do all day, and it is no wonder he is classed as a genius."

Despite W. O. Wolfe's failing health, he and Mrs. Wolfe were determined to make the trip to Chapel Hill for their son's graduation from college. Wolfe noted in his *Autobiographical Outline for Look Homeward, Angel* (ed. Lucy Conniff and Richard S. Kennedy [Baton Rouge: Louisiana State University Press, 2004]): "Papas illness . . .—On his last legs but with two more years to live—The room I found for them . . .—The suit I bought in Durham—Chase's [Harry Woodburn Chase, president of the university] whispered word to papa" (57).

W. O. Wolfe heard his son's presentation of the class gift on Monday morning, June 14; that afternoon at 5:30, during the "Closing of the Senior Class under the Davie Poplar," Thomas Wolfe read the class poem, "1920 Says a Few Words to Carolina," in which he looked ahead to the day when members of his class would "think again of Chapel Hill and— / Thinking—come back home."

A.P.M.

North Carolina Collection, University of North Carolina at Chapel Hill

YACKETY YACK
'20

VOLUME XXX

Published Annually by
The Dialectic and Philanthropic Literary Societies
and The Fraternities of the
UNIVERSITY OF NORTH CAROLINA
CHAPEL HILL, N. C.

1920 Says a Few Words to Carolina

We stand 'round the well in the white gleaming
   moonlight
And look at the square of the buildings old,
And sharp is the thought of tomorrow; tonight
Is the last—ah—we've been told
How hard it was, but not till now
Have we felt the deep twisting pain of the parting
From you—Carolina—we did not allow
For the deep biting grief that now we feel starting.

Yet it's not the old buildings that causes the
   pain
(You brown, dirty buildings—and God knows
   that's true),
But comes back the feeling again and again
That we part from a friend—Carolina, it's you.
You cared not for sects or for social degree;
You care not for dogmas or creeds now as then;
You take the crude stuff and you fashion it free,
Till shapen and moulded you send forth your
   men.

Tomorrow we leave—1920, your War Class,
A class proud in deeds in a war that was won,
A mixture of warrior and student—we pass,
The warfaring student salutes, and is gone,
Leaving State's mantle to those just below;
Pausing to listen as South's slow toll rings,
Then quickens as to our successors we bow,
For—"The kings having gone—long live the
   kings!"

Ah! sometimes from the straight white path
Our stumbling steps may stray;
And sometimes where the hillside slopes
We'll choose the easier way;
And sometimes when the path is rough
That takes us straight through life,
Our strength will fail, and craven-like,
We'll shun the bitter strife,
To choose the broad and paven road,
And eat the lotus leaf.

Yes, some will fail and take this road,
For grinding toil and grief

Are on the sterner road you point,
With hand in hand their mate,
Good Manhood, walking true and brave
Along the path that's straight.
Yes, some will falter on this road
And choose the broader way,
But when again the soft nights come
And Spring has come to stay,
They'll think perhaps of this last night—
The Campus white and still,
The dorms, the well, the old South bell—
Of all that's on the "Hill",
And then they'll leave the broader path
That leads to life's ill wrack,
To seek again the narrow one and—
Finding it—come back.

To some will fall the ivy wreath
That marks the place of fame,
While some will plod along beneath
The peaks of greatest name;
The years will pass and very faint
Will be your call to these,
For time is scornful of the past
And ever onward flees.
But sometimes when the Springtime comes,
And the sifting moonlight falls—
They'll think again of this night here
And of these old brown walls,
Of white old well, and of old South
With bell's deep booming tone,
They'll think again of Chapel Hill and—
Thinking—come back home.

L'ENVOI

(Again '20 talks to Carolina)
Some say that God worked six days hard
And made the world for man—
But on the seventh rested.
We have a better plan—
For, being God he was not tired;
This is the broader view,
God made the world in six days—
The seventh, he made You!

                            T. C. WOLFE

The Return of Buck Gavin:
The Tragedy of a Mountain Outlaw, 1919

In *Carolina Folk-Plays, Second Series,* edited by Frederick H. Koch (New York: Henry Holt, 1924), 30–44

By the time Frederick Henry Koch came to the University of North Carolina in 1918, he had established himself as a successful instructor of folk-drama composition at the University of North Dakota. Then fifty years old, a dapper figure who dressed in a tweed Norfolk jacket and a Windsor tie, he insisted on being called Proff ("And be sure to spell it with a double-*f*!"). Since most of the male population was involved in SATC (Students' Army Training Corps), his first playwriting class at Chapel Hill consisted of eight females and one male, Thomas Wolfe. When Koch seemed disappointed that only one male had registered for the class, Wolfe explained, "Proff, I don't want you to think that this Ladies' Aid Society represents Carolina. We have a lot of he-men seriously writing here, but they're all disguised in uniforms now. I tried to get myself into one myself but they didn't have one to fit me" (Walser, *Thomas Wolfe Undergraduate,* 87).

When Wolfe's first attempts at playwriting failed, he turned to Proff Koch for a suitable subject. From his folder marked "Play Ideas," Koch gave Wolfe a clipping from the *Grand Forks Herald* (June 10, 1906) with a story head-lined "To Place Flowers on Pal's Grave—Outlaw Lavin Seeks to Honor His Comrade and Is Nabbed by Police." He suggested Wolfe adapt the play with folk characters from and with a background in the North Carolina mountains. It struck Wolfe as a daunting assignment since he had lived all his life in Asheville and knew little of rural mountain life.

In the real story, following a bank robbery Charles Coleman and his friend Patrick Lavin, known in Texas as the bank robber Cyclone Pat, were apprehended by the sheriff's posse and, in a shoot-out, Coleman's body was riddled with a hundred bullets. Lavin, who made his escape in the darkness, was later arrested in the Chicago home of his sister. He had returned to the city hoping to place daisies on Charles Coleman's grave. After his arrest he asked the sheriff for permission to pay someone to place the flowers on the grave for him.

In Wolfe's treatment of the newspaper story, Patrick Lavin becomes Buck Gavin, the leader of a mountain clan who is a fugitive from justice and wanted on charges of moonshining and murder. In a shootout with the sheriff's posse, his friend is killed but Buck escapes. After eluding the posse for six weeks, he returns to his cabin in the Carolina mountains, where he finds his sister Mary, who tells him his friend "Jim Preas" is buried "'top o' big Smoky." He asks his sister to pick some violets (Wolfe's favorite flower) for him to take to his friend's grave. Gavin is apprehended by the sheriff just as Mary arrives with a bunch of violets. Buck goes quietly with the sheriff but tells his sister to place the flowers on Jim's grave for him: "I would've liked to 've took 'em up there, an' . . . an' . . . sort o' looked 'round. But . . . well, I reckon I cain't go now . . . but ol' Jim'll know . . . jes' the same, Sis,—you take 'em."

In "Thomas Wolfe—Playmaker," Koch recalled that at tryouts for casting Buck Gavin no one volunteered to play the leading role. When Koch told Wolfe he would have to play the part and that he had really written the part for himself, Wolfe responded, "I've never acted." "You're a born actor," Koch replied, "and you *are* Buck Gavin" (*Carolina Play-Book* 8 [June 1935]: 36).

The Return of Buck Gavin, along with two other one-act plays, was presented on March 15 and 16, 1919, in the Chapel Hill High School auditorium. The play was a success, and Wolfe made a striking impression in the title role. Though in later years Wolfe downplayed *Buck Gavin* as something he tossed off in several hours on a rainy afternoon, there is truth in Richard Walser's assessment that "certainly no masterwork, 'The Return of Buck Gavin' was even so a commendable effort for an eighteen-year-old" (*Thomas Wolfe Undergraduate,* 94).

The Return of Buck Gavin was first published in *Carolina Folk-Plays, Second Series,* later in *Carolina Folk-Plays, First, Second, and Third Series,* edited by Frederick H. Koch (New York: Henry Holt, 1924 and 1941), and still later in *North Carolina Drama,* edited by Richard Walser (Richmond: Garrett and Massie, 1956).

A.P.M.

The Return of Buck Gavin

THE CHARACTERS
As originally produced on The Playmakers' Stage, Chapel Hill, North Carolina, March 14th and 15th, 1919.

BUCK GAVIN, *a mountain outlaw,* . . . . Thomas Clayton Wolfe
MARY GAVIN, *his sister,* . . . . Lelia Nance Moffatt
THE SHERIFF, ... Frederick Cohn

Thomas Wolfe
as Buck Gavin
in *The Return of
Buck Gavin.* North
Carolina Collec-
tion, University of
North Carolina at
Chapel Hill

SCENE: The cabin home of Buck Gavin in a remote cove of the Carolina mountains.

TIME: The present. An afternoon in May.

SCENE

The living and dining room of the log cabin home of Buck Gavin.

The furnishings of the room are more pretentious than are usually associated with mountain cabins. This is explained by the fact that Gavin is a mountain chief, the leader of a clan—a kind of tribal leader, if you like. The interior is rude, but comfortable, with not a little taste displayed in the arrangement. A woman's presence is denoted by blue chintz curtains at the windows and a covering of the same material on the table in the center of the room. A shaded lamp, several weekly newspapers, and a knitting basket are on the table. At the left a crackling wood-fire burns in a large stone fire-place. In the right corner is a home-made cupboard. Skins are tacked to the wall here and there. The garish lithographic display usually found in moun-tain cabins is lacking here. Several hand-made, splint-bottom chairs are grouped around the hearth. The outside door is in the rear wall at the cen-ter, with small windows on either side of it. In the right wall is another door, leading into the bedroom and thence into the kitchen shed. There is a rocker by the table.

Mary Gavin is seated in this rocker, knitting. She has a face not old, but worn—not by toil, we should say, but care-worn. It is a good face—attractive, possessing a sensitiveness of feature remarkable for a mountain woman. Although she is not more than thirty-five years of age, her hair is even now streaked with gray. As she knits, her back to the door, it opens softly, slowly. A man steps quickly into the room and shuts the door as quietly as it was opened. The man is Buck Gavin, master of the house, a fugitive from justice, wanted on charges of illicit distilling and murder. He has returned by stealth after being hunted for six weeks.

Buck Gavin is a great, powerfully built fellow, aged forty years, or thereabouts. He has a strong, heavily-lined face, covered by a beard of the Van Dyke type—although he would not call it that. He has piercing black eyes and heavy black hair. In his swift silent movements there is a suggestion of a veiled panther-like power. This seems characteristic of him; he moves always with the same decisiveness. He is dressed in a dark flannel shirt and loose corduroy trousers stuffed into rough laced boots.

GAVIN

(Stands quietly a moment surveying the scene; then he speaks casually, quietly)

Howdy, sis.

MARY

(Springing from her chair and turning quickly)

Buck! Buck! My God! What air you doin' here? Why did you come back?

GAVIN

(Simply)

I had to, sis.

MARY

But, my Lor', man, they've been lookin' fer you high an' low. There's nary a nook ner corner 'bout these hills they haven't scoured fer you.

GAVIN

Don't you reckon I know it? But I come, an' thar's an end to it. (*Speaking impatiently as she starts to interrupt him.*) Don't argue with me. I come . . . an' you know why, I'm thinkin'.

MARY

(Sullenly)

Yeah. I calc'late I knowed why. (*Going to him.*) But 'twarn't no use, Buck, 'twarn't no use for you to risk yer neck after all's over.

GAVIN

(With quiet emphasis)

Thar's the rub. 'Tain't all over. There's one mo' leetle job to be done, an' I reckon I'll git to see that through . . . least-ways, I'd better. For they'd never o' caught me whar I was, an' I don't calc'late to come more'n two hundred miles jes' to be caught. I reckon they'll git me soon, anyway; they're so powerful smart.

MARY

(Contemptuously and proudly)

Bah! They never could o' caught you in the ol' days, Buck, no matter how powerful smart they were. You'd allus fool 'em, Buck.

GAVIN

The ol' days is gone—the good ol' days—an' all that made 'em good. But now . . . now . . . well, I'm jes' not in the foolin' mood. (*Moving away from her.*) . . . He's gone . . . they got him, an' I'd ruther that it'd been me. I reckon you know it. . . . But they got him, damn 'em, an' now . . . now . . . (*Passionately.*) Aw, what's the use? (*Striding restlessly across the room.*) A lot I'd keer if they'd come now . . . only . . . only . . . I want a leetle mo' time . . . jes' a leetle.

MARY

Buck! Buck! Perk up, man, you mustn't act this way. What's come over you?

GAVIN

Oh, don't worry 'bout me. . . . (*He speaks softly.*) Where'd you put him, Mary?

MARY

On the top o' big Smoky. You know he allus liked the view up there . . . said kind o' jokin' that that was where he wanted 'em to plant him.

GAVIN

(Almost in a whisper)

I . . . rec'lect.

MARY

So the rest o' the boys built a kind o' box an' carried him up there. 'Twarn't easy neither, for it's a good ten mile from the Gap to the top o' the Smoky. But we all felt sort o' like it was doin' the right thing by Jim. Allus was different, was Jim, from the rest of us. He'd have them dreamy times when he wanted to be left alone.

GAVIN

(Sits down at the table and gazes before him)

He was plumb foolish over the view from the Smoky. Called it a leetle bit o' God's country. Used to go up there an' stare off 'cross the valleys till the sun got low an' everythin' was blurred an' hazy-like. Didn't want to talk to no one when he got that-a-way. But one time, when we was up there, he set a-lookin' out awhile an' he turned to me an' says, says he, "Buck, this is shore purty. We're powerful close to heaven, Buck. . . . " I reckon you done the right thing to plant him there. . . . Good ol' Jim. It's 'bout all we could do. But the best warn't good 'nough fer him.

MARY

On the box we carved out his name . . . jes' carved "Jim." Somehow it seemed more nat'ral-like to have it "Jim" than "James Preas." An' over the grave—at the head, I mean—we stuck a wooden cross that the boys made . . . an' on it we carved "Jim Preas—He asked no favors from revenooers an' he died with his boots off."

GAVIN

(Sharply)

What's that 'bout his boots?

MARY

Oh, that's the funny part of it. He had his leetle joke right to the end. You know he allus calc'lated he'd have his boots off when he died. Well, when the Sheriff an' his dep'ties found him, he was lyin' up agin' a rock with his boots off, with his gun in one hand, an' grinnin' a funny leetle grin as if he was sayin', "I had the last laugh, hey?"

GAVIN

(Quietly after a pause)

How . . . how many did we git?

MARY

Three dep'ties.

GAVIN

(With savage satisfaction)

Good . . . good, damn 'em, they had to pay. A lot o' good it does me, though. (He goes on reminiscently.) I won't forgit the fight out there on the hill-side, an' how they got him. He gives a funny leetle cough an' crumples up an' quits pumpin' his gun. "Buck," he says, grinnin' that crooked grin of his'n, "Buck, my boy, I reckon they've settled my hash. . . . 'Tain't no use, big feller," says he when I starts to carry him, "They've got me, an' I'm done fer. You can't help me, so for God's sake, help yourself. Now git." So I left him jokin' an' grinnin' an' pumpin' lead at 'em. He was a great joker, was Jim. . . . (They are both silent.) Mary, I reckon I ought to git some flowers. Could you git 'em fer me?

MARY

(Puzzled by the question)

Why, yeah, I reckon I could. I got some here picked fresh this mornin', but what on airth d'you want . . . Buck, you can't be meanin' to go up there with 'em. Why, man alive, you cain't—they're searchin' high an' low fer you.

GAVIN

(Doggedly)

No matter if they air—I'm goin'. That's what I come fer.

CAROLINA PLAYMAKERS
Present First Program
Fri. and Sat. Nights

The first performance of the Carolina Playmakers will be presented in the auditorium of the Chapel Hill School on the nights of March 14 and 15 successively. The curtain will be raised promptly at eight o'clock. Professor Koch and others in charge of the performance are hopeful of filling the "theatre" each night. All seats will be reserved and will be on sale at Eubank's Drug Store at the price of fifty cents early in the week.

The program will be divided in two parts, first the play of college life, "What Will Barbara Say?" by Minnie Shepherd Sparrow, and then two folk plays,—"The Return of Buck Gavin," by Thomas Wolfe, and "When Witches Ride," by Elizabeth A. Lay.

Music will be rendered by the University Orchestra between the plays and incidental music on the guitar and mandolin will be a feature of the college atmosphere of "What Will Barbara Say?"

Rehearsals of all the plays has been going on steadily for the past two weeks so that the school auditorium has been in almost constant use every afternoon and night. In the basement room below the scene painting department has been working steadily on a canvas setting, a log cabin for use in the folk plays. Stage construction under Professor Rankin's direction has been going forward at the same time and the movable panel setting is now in place on the stage and the columns which finish the sides of the stage have been erected in position. Special reflectors for the foot lights have been constructed by Professor Lear with arrangements for manufacturing stage thunder and lightning and color effects for the plays. The school house is the scene of real community play making in which every branch is being worked out by "home talent."

The pictures of the plays will be taken Thursday and the full rehearsal with lights and music will take place Wednesday night.

The full casts of the plays follows:
"What Will Barbara Say?"—by Minnie Shepherd Sparrow.

Graduate students at the University of North Carolina:
Marguerite Davis, sociologist—Mary Polk Beard.
Martha McIlwaine, biologist—Mabel Brooks.
Frances Merrimon, lawyer—Louisa P. Reid.
Barbara Grey, Ph. D.—Minnie S. Sparrow.
Tom, Marguerite's suitor—Jonathan Daniels.
Smithy, Martha's suitor—Ernest Neiman.

(Continued on Page 4)

(Continued from Page 1)

Bill, Frances' suitor—Albert Oettinger.
Mr. Sanderson, Professor of Sociology, in love with Barbara—Arthur Spaugh.
Rosetta, the maid—Sally Vick Whitfield.
Potter, the man—Chester Burton.
Dr. Moss, the parson—John Lasley.
Minerva—William Goforth.
Cupid—Edward Kidder Graham.
"The Return of Buck Gavin"—by Thomas Wolfe.
Buck Gavin, a mountain outlaw—Thomas Wolfe.
Mary, his sister—Mrs. James Moffat.
The sheriff—Frederick H. Cohn.
"When Witches Ride"—by Elizabeth A. Lay.
Uncle Benny, owner of the crossroads general store—George McKee.
Ed, his son—W. H. Williamson.
Jake—George Denny.
Phoebe Ward, witch—Mrs. S. C. Leavitt.

Production Department

Producing Committee: Professors McKie and Bernard, Mrs. S. E. Leavitt.
Director of Stage-Craft: Professor P. H. Daggett.
Director of Lighting: Professor Lear.
Director of Construction: Professor Rankin.
Director of Scene Painting: Miss Pritchard.
Mistress of Wardrobe: Mrs. J. H. Pratt.
Stage Settings and Properties: Professor Lasley, Mrs. Doy, Miss Love.
Business Manager: Mr. C. T. Woolen.
House Manager: Prof. Wheeler.
Ass't Stage Manager: Chester Burton.
Director of Orchestra: E. S. Lindsey.
Director of Publicity: W. R. Wunsch.
Scene Painting: Misses Pritchard, Lay, Thornton and Kennette. Messrs. Thornton, Sumner and Coker.

Tar Heel, March 7, 1919. North Carolina Collection, University of North Carolina at Chapel Hill

Thomas Wolfe as Buck Gavin. North Carolina Collection, University of North Carolina at Chapel Hill

MARY

D'you mean to tell me, Buck Gavin, that you come all this way to risk your neck fer . . . fer . . . sech? . . .

GAVIN

(With quiet determination)

Yeah, I mean to tell you jes' that. That's what kep' pullin' me home; that's all I hanker to do an' after that's done let 'em come an' git me . . . an' to hell with 'em.

MARY

All right, Buck, I reckon you know. I'll git 'em.

GAVIN

(To himself)

With his boots off, hey? (*He sits down at the table.*) By cripes, that was like him, jes' like ol' Jim. Allus was a joker. (*He chuckles.*) I reckon that tickled him. Oh, Lord, that was a man fer you!

(He rises and strides across the room.)

MARY

(Returning with a large bunch of arbutus)

Reckon these'll do, Buck?

GAVIN

Guess so—too many, though. Here, le' me have 'em, I'll fix 'em. Say, how 'bout some vi'lets, got any? Jim was plumb daffy over 'em—the big blue uns. You know the kind, Mary?

MARY

I know where they's a sight of 'em. I'll go git 'em. 'Twon't take long.

(She goes out.)

GAVIN

(Sitting by the table, he speaks disjointedly as he arranges the flowers)

No, an' 'twon't take long fer you either, Gavin, my boy. . . . Your goose is 'bout cooked, I'm thinkin'. Fine way of cookin', too. Jim's was the right way after all. . . . Wish I'd stayed with him now. A purty sight I'll be with a noose 'round my gullet—first Gavin to be hung—a disgrace to the family. . . . They'll git me—they allus git us. We've fit 'em time an' time, an' they git us in the end. Lord, I reckon we'uns is all fools. . . . *(Holding the bunch of arbutus at arm's length.)* . . . There, that's purty now.

(Now the door opens slowly and a short, thick-set fellow steps into the room. The badge of an officer of the law can be seen under his coat. In his hand he holds a revolver. He is the SHERIFF.*)*

THE SHERIFF

(Smiling ironically)

Welcome home, Buck.

*(*GAVIN *wheels swiftly, his hand moving to his hip pocket. He stops short on seeing the* SHERIFF's *gun.)*

GAVIN

Aw. . . . Hell. . . .

THE SHERIFF

(Genially, highly pleased with himself)

Quite a surprise, eh? Knew you'd be back, my boy, so I jes' laid low fer you. You never had a chance.

GAVIN

(Slowly)

Yeah, you got me I reckon, Sheriff, but I ain't worryin' 'bout it. Fact is, I'm glad you come—only . . . only I wish to God you'd been a leetle later.

THE SHERIFF

(Surprised)

Why?

GAVIN

(Sullenly)

Aw . . . nothin'. Come on, let's be travelin'. My sister'll be back any minute now, an' I don't want her to see the kind o' company I've took up with.

THE SHERIFF

(In a high good humor)

Jes' as you say, Buck, jes' as you say.

(They start toward the door as MARY *enters with a large bunch of violets. She sums up the situation at a glance.)*

MARY

Oh, Buck, Buck, why did you come? I told you. An' now they've got you. I knowed it!

(She sinks into a chair and buries her face in her hands.)

GAVIN

(He speaks gently and clumsily tries to soothe her)

There, there, little sis, you mustn't carry on so. This is sartin' the best way out an' I'm not worr'in'—look at me. I'm glad, sis. What's in the game fer me now? My pal's gone an' there ain't no mo' fun in playin' it without him. . . . Tell the boys hello an' good-by fer me, an' tell 'em I says—But you needn't t' mind. . . . As fer you . . . (*Going to her.*) . . . you needn't to worry 'bout nothin' no mo'. I've fixed things up fer you.

MARY

Oh Buck, you needn't o' been caught. You could've got away.

GAVIN

(With quiet emphasis)

It is the law. You cain't buck it. (*There is a pause. The* SHERIFF *stands with bowed head, his jesting spirit gone. Then* GAVIN *speaks awkwardly as he prepares to leave.*) Well, I reckon that's about all, so I'll be a-goin'. Be good to yourself, sis.

(*He notices the arbutus and the violets on the table and picks them up, muttering under his breath.*) I would've liked to 've took 'em up there, an' . . . an' . . . sort o' looked 'round. (*He looks at* MARY, *deeply moved.*) But . . . well, I reckon I cain't go now . . . but ol' Jim'll know . . . jes' the same. Sis,—you take 'em.

(He places the flowers in her lap. MARY *does not raise her head. He pats her hair gently, clumsily, once or twice, then turns to go with the* SHERIFF. *At the door he turns and gives a last look around the room. His gaze rests finally on his sister. Then he goes out quietly.* MARY'S *head is pillowed in her arms. The flowers are in her lap.*

SLOW CURTAIN

The Third Night: A Play of the Carolina Mountains, 1919

Carolina Play-Book of the Carolina Playmakers and the Carolina Dramatic Association 11, no. 3 (September 1938): 70–75

The Third Night, the second and last of Wolfe's plays staged by the Carolina Playmakers, was presented at the Chapel Hill High School auditorium on December 12 and 13, 1919, with the author in the role of Captain Richard Harkins, "a degenerate Southern gentleman." In his usual rush to meet deadlines, Wolfe wrote this play quickly, just as he had *The Return of Buck Gavin.*

Less successful than *Buck Gavin,* this new play, somewhat static and talky, was freely adapted from Lord Dunsany's play *A Night at the Inn.* The setting of the play is the living room of a dilapidated dwelling in a deserted mountain area of North Carolina, "some miles west of Asheville," on a stormy night in the autumn of 1858. It is the third night after Harkins has robbed and killed the father of the girl he had not been allowed to marry. The ghost of the dead man appears and leads Harkins to destruction. The play meets the criteria delineated by Professor Koch in his playwriting class and later delineated by Wolfe in his article on Koch ("The Man Who Lives with His Idea") that folk drama primarily be "written from character types known in person to the author and from scenes familiar to the writer's own experience," or, as Walser says, "a play of the *people* coming from the soil" (*Thomas Wolfe Undergraduate,* 88).

As Walser observes about the plays written during Wolfe's junior year at Chapel Hill, "Amateurish they may have been, but Wolfe was so pleased by their reception that he began to dream of the day when he would be able to write plays with professional competence" (*Thomas Wolfe Undergraduate,* 97). With that dream in mind and the encouragement of Frederick Koch, upon graduation from Chapel Hill, Wolfe left to study playwriting with George Pierce Baker, the prestigious drama professor at Harvard.

A.P.M.

The Third Night

A Play of the Carolina Mountains

By Thomas Wolfe

❡ A HITHERTO UNPUBLISHED work of Thomas Wolfe written when he was a student in the playwriting course at the University of North Carolina nearly twenty years ago. "The Third Night" was produced by The Carolina Playmakers on their original improvised stage in the auditorium of the Chapel Hill high school building on December 12 and 13, 1919.

THE CHARACTERS

CAPTAIN RICHARD HARKINS, *a degenerate Southern gentleman*............................THE AUTHOR
DORSET, *his henchman*..Jonathan Daniels
COGSWELL, *a mulatto*..Fred Cohn
THE OLD MAN...Chester Burton

SCENE: The living room of a dilapidated dwelling of the "Old Man" in a deserted mountain section of North Carolina, some miles west of Asheville.

TIME: A stormy night in the autumn of 1858.

❡ *The gloomy living room of a decaying country house in a dark mountain valley of the Blue Ridge. The plaster is cracked; great patches of it have fallen from the high ceiling. The rear wall is broken by a single uncurtained window at the right and an open doorway at the left, through which another room is partly visible. At the right, downstage, is an ample fireplace with a rude table and two chairs before it. A door at the left leads outside.*

❡ *A smouldering fagot gives a half light to the bare, gaunt room; the corners are almost in darkness. Before the fireplace in the room at the rear* THE CAPTAIN *is sitting, his profile silhouetted by the glow of the hearth.*

❡ COGSWELL *and* DORSET *are seated at the table.* COGSWELL *is playing a game of solitaire with a pack of greasy cards.* DORSET *is thumbing the pages of a well-worn family photograph album with an air of detached curiosity. The light is just sufficient to accentuate the lines of each man's face.* COGSWELL'S, *the face of the degenerate, is weak but sensitive and mobile. He is a young man, half negro. In him have cumulated many of the superstitions of the black race.* DORSET *is thickset, unemotional, unexpressive—ox-like, as he sits in squat stolidity, thumbing the pages of the album with pudgy fingers. He looks over at* COGSWELL *out of his little, pig-like eyes. The two men are strongly contrasted.* DORSET *speaks ponderously with a slow drawl,* COGSWELL *with nervous rapidity. Both are roughly dressed. They are without coats and wear heavy boots.* COGSWELL *is smooth-faced;* DORSET *has a short, unkempt beard.*

❡ *The Third Night copyrighted 1938 by The Carolina Playmakers, Inc. All rights reserved.*

Carolina Play-Book, September 1938

The Third Night

A Play of the Carolina Mountains

BY THOMAS WOLFE

A hitherto unpublished work of Thomas Wolfe written when he was a student in the playwriting course at the University of North Carolina nearly twenty years ago. "The Third Night" was produced by The Carolina Playmakers on their original improvised stage in the auditorium of the Chapel Hill high school building on December 12 and 13, 1919.

THE CHARACTERS

CAPTAIN RICHARD HARKINS,
a degenerate Southern gentleman .... The Author
DORSET, his henchman........................... Jonathan Daniels
COGSWELL, a mulatto .... Fred Cohn
THE OLD MAN................................... Chester Burton

SCENE: The living room of a dilapidated dwelling of the "Old Man" in a
deserted mountain section of North Carolina, some miles west of
Asheville.

TIME: A stormy night in the autumn of 1858.

The gloomy living room of a decaying country house in a dark mountain
valley of the Blue Ridge. The plaster is cracked; great patches of it have fallen
from the high ceiling. The rear wall is broken by a single uncurtained window at the right and an open doorway at the left, through which another
room is partly visible. At the right, downstage, is an ample fireplace with a
rude table and two chairs before it. A door at the left leads outside.

A smouldering fagot gives a half light to the bare, gaunt room; the corners are almost in darkness. Before the fireplace in the room at the rear THE
CAPTAIN is sitting, his profile silhouetted by the glow of the hearth.

COGSWELL and DORSET are seated at the table. COGSWELL is playing a
game of solitaire with a pack of greasy cards. DORSET is thumbing the pages
of a well-worn family photograph album with an air of detached curiosity. The
light is just sufficient to accentuate the lines of each man's face. COGSWELL's,
the face of the degenerate, is weak but sensitive and mobile. He is a young
man, half negro. In him have cumulated many of the superstitions of the
black race. DORSET is thickset, unemotional, unexpressive—ox-like, as he
sits in squat stolidity, thumbing the pages of the album with pudgy fingers.
He looks over at COGSWELL out of his little, pig-like eyes. The two men are
strongly contrasted. DORSET speaks ponderously with a slow drawl, COGSWELL
with nervous rapidity. Both are roughly dressed. They are without coats and
wear heavy boots. COGSWELL is smooth-faced; DORSET has a short, unkempt
beard.

There is a dark silence except for the moaning of the storm outside.
COGSWELL plays a card or two.

DORSET. [*Thumbing the album.*] This is the third night, ain't it, an' we're
still here.

COGSWELL. [*Looking up with a nervous start, as he puts down a card on the
table.*] The third—the *third*, you say? The third . . . since we done it?

DORSET. Sure. Had you lost track?

COGSWELL. The third—that's bad; we should 'a' left befo'.

DORSET. That's the Cap'n—that quair way of his'n. [*He motions toward
the door at the rear—then turns to* COGSWELL, *eyeing him intently.*] What's
wrong, Cogswell? We're right enough here, ain't we?

COGSWELL. [*Half embarrassed.*] I reckon . . . only—God, Dorset, listen to
that rain . . . listen to that wind howl!

DORSET. [*Indifferently.*] Yeah. Purty bad storm, I reckon.

[*There is silence for a moment.* DORSET *turns a page in the album.*]

[THE CAPTAIN *enters. He is very tall and slenderly built, fashionably dressed in the style of his period. He is a dark, handsome man of aristocratic bearing and fine, but somewhat dissipated, features. He wears a well-groomed moustache.*]

[*He goes to the window and looks out at the storm, then turns, looks intently with sinister foreboding at* COGSWELL *and* DORSET, *and goes back into the rear room.*]

COGSWELL. I don't like the way he acts.

DORSET. He don't mean nothin'. 'S his way, you know.

COGSWELL. [*After a pause.*] What's that book you're readin'?

DORSET. 'Tain't no book. It's a album.

COGSWELL. What's that?

DORSET. You put picters of yer folks in it—a photygraph album, they calls it.

COGSWELL. [*In a subdued voice.*] Was it . . . was it the . . . Old Man's?

DORSET. Yeah, I reckon. Found it upstairs while I was rummagin' 'round today. Found his picter in it—a lot of 'em. See here—[*He pushes the album over to* COGSWELL *and traces with his finger.*] Here's one with "sixteen" under it—this boy, you see here—that's the old duck at sixteen. Another'n here at twenty-three. Here's one at forty—you can tell him here all right.

COGSWELL. [*With a shiver.*] Yeah, that's him . . . that's him . . . he was a lot older but y' can tell that's him, all right. [*He shudders.*] I can't forgit how the ol' bird looked when the Cap'n killed him, how he laughed all up in his throat when the Cap'n shot him . . . a bloody gurgle it were.

DORSET. [*Bluntly.*] Forgit it. I ought to 'a' been here to do it for you an' not a-traipsin' down the mountain for grub that night.

COGSWELL. [*Not heeding.*] An' the funny part is that he knew the Cap'n—

DORSET. [*Staring at him in astonishment.*] What's that?—You're crazy!— Knew the Cap'n? Why he couldn't. He ain't never been in these parts before. Said he hadn't.

COGSWELL. [*Glancing nervously toward the rear room where* THE CAPTAIN *is pacing up and down.*] He did all the same, he spoke his name.

[THE CAPTAIN *comes to the open door. He pauses a moment and looks into the front room—a cynical, half-brooding look. The men sense his presence. They are silent but glance nervously at each other and fidget under his gaze, not daring to look up until he retires.*]

COGSWELL. [*Looking craftily toward the door before he speaks.*] Damn him! I wish he wouldn't look at us like that. 'Tain't like he's human. No, it ain't.

Thomas Wolfe (right) as Captain Richard Harkins in *The Third Night.* North Carolina Collection, University of North Carolina at Chapel Hill

DORSET. [*Defending his chief.*] He's all right . . . [*There is a pause.*] You say the Ol' Man spoke the Cap'n's name? Tell me about it. I wa'n't in here when it happened.

COGSWELL. The first thing that struck me funny was the noise the Cap'n made when he come in. An' him knowin' all the time that the Ol' Man was asleep upstairs. Right over his head!

DORSET. [*Unbelieving.*] You say he made a noise, an' him as soft-steppin' as a cat?

COGSWELL. I know, I know, but he did. Went clumpin' over the floor like no one was 'round, like he didn't care. I says "Cap'n, be keerful, you'll wake the Ol' Man."

DORSET. What did he say?

COGSWELL. Nothin'. He looked at me an' grinned that mean little grin of his'n. 'Bout that time th' ol' bird heard us. He hit the floor an' come thumpin' down the stairs . . . thought we were after his money, an' he wa'n't far wrong. I tell you he was a funny sight in his night shirt, an' his red night cap, an' his ol' shanks like two sticks as he come down a-glarin' at us.

DORSET. [*Almost eagerly.*] Go on, man. The Cap'n, the Cap'n—what did he do?

COGSWELL. When he heard the Ol' Un' comin', he turned his back.

DORSET. What?

COGSWELL. Yeah, that he did! An' then the Ol' Un' come down the stairs into the room an' started screamin', "What do you want? Who are you? Burglars, by God!" An' he ran over to the stone where his money is . . .

DORSET. [*Impatiently.*] Go on, go on!

COGSWELL. The Cap'n turned an' faced him, never sayin' a word. An' the Ol' Un's eyes nearly popped out'n his head—he was that put to it . . .

DORSET. What did the Cap'n do then?

COGSWELL. In a minute th' Ol' Man croaked out, "Richard Harkins— Richard Harkins—Richard Harkins!"

DORSET. An' the Cap'n, what did he say?

COGSWELL. Nothin'. Jes' grinned his mean grin, the one that makes you fidgety, you know.

DORSET. [*Dully.*] Yeah, I know. . . . Go on, Cogswell.

COGSWELL. Finally the Ol' Man starts laughin', jes' stands there laughin' . . . a gaspin', gurglin' kind o' laugh . . . make yo' blood freeze.

DORSET. Didn't he talk none?

COGSWELL. Yeah. Finally he says, still laughin', "I fooled you, didn't I, Captain Richard Harkins; I fooled you, hey? You thought you'd take her but I fooled you. An' now she's gone, she's dead. I took her away from you an' she died, she died!" An' with that he started laughin' his bloody laugh again. The Cap'n shot him then. Standin' still an' cold as ice, the Cap'n shot him through the neck. He fell still laughin'—right by that stone where his money is. [*He shudders as the recollection.*]

DORSET. Yeah, I know. I was comin' back when I heard the shot an' I hurried in. The blood spots are still there—but why didn't you tell me this before, Cogswell? Why didn't you?

[THE CAPTAIN *is heard pacing in the adjoining room.*]

COGSWELL. [*Whining now, as he gazes in that direction.*] It was him, damn him! I'm afeard o' him an' the way he looked at me that night, an' I swore to myself I wouldn't tell no one if I got out of here. But—[*Listening to the rain as it drives against the house.*] God, Dorset, this is the third night! [*He is almost whimpering as his overstrained nerves give way.*] The Cap'n done it,

Dorset; I didn't know 'bout it or I wouldn't 'a' come along. The Cap'n killed him, Dorset. It wa'n't no work o' mine, Dorset, and this is the third night. . . . We oughtn't to be here!

DORSET. [*Eyeing him curiously.*] What's in the third business, Cogswell?

COGSWELL. Third is bad all the time. On the third night the hoot owl screeches; the third time the dog barks; the third night—

DORSET. Bah! That's the nigger in you showin' up. [COGSWELL *springs up furiously with clenched fist, but in a moment sinks sullenly back into his chair, cowed by* DORSET'S *threatening contempt.* DORSET *turns away, meditating with his sluggish mind on* COGSWELL'S *account of the killing. While* COGSWELL *fools nervously with the cards, he turns the pages of the album, muttering.*] The Ol' Man talked of a girl, huh . . . that's funny . . . damn funny—[*Half indifferently.*] Now, I wonder . . . [*Suddenly he stiffens in his seat as his glance rests on a certain photograph in the album. He speaks hoarsely.*] Good God! The picture, the locket picture; it's the girl!

COGSWELL. [*Frightened, stares at him.*] What . . . what do you mean?

DORSET. [*Excited.*] Here it is! . . . Why didn't I see it when you tol' me 'bout the Ol' Man's talk of the girl . . . an' him knowin' the Cap'n?

COGSWELL. What . . . what are you talkin' 'bout?

DORSET. The Cap'n carries a locket 'round his neck. Got a girl's picter in it. When he's drinkin' he takes it out an' curses under his breath, slow an' soft an' steady—awful, I tell you.

COGSWELL. He's drinkin' now.

DORSET. An' it's the same as this picter here, the Ol' Man's daughter. . . . Don't you see, Cogswell? It's plain as the nose on your face. [COGSWELL *shakes his head.*]

DORSET. Why the Cap'n come back to kill 'im. That's what he come for. Why, I don't even believe he wanted his money. The Ol' Man must've took his daughter away from the Cap'n long ago. Don't you see?

COGSWELL. [*In an awed tone.*] God, Dorset, is that it?—How long you been with that man, Dorset?

DORSET. Five year. He picked me up in Memphis. Five year last week it was, when we picked you up in Asheville.

COGSWELL. [*Interrupting.*] I had nothin' to do with it, I tell you. I never knew there was to be a killin'. I just come to show you the way.

DORSET. [*Grinning at him.*] Yes, you did. You'd heard of the Ol' Man's money, that's what you wanted.

COGSWELL. [*Sullenly.*] Well, mebbe you're right. . . . But it wa'n't no work o' mine.

DORSET. [*Taunting him.*] Anxious to git out of it, ain't you?

COGSWELL. [*Whining again.*] You would be too, if you knew all 'bout the Ol' Man.

DORSET. What's that?

COGSWELL. [*Lowering his voice and glancing around nervously.*] They say 'round here he was a witch-man—half-way crazy, he was. Whenever anything went wrong with farmers or when there was a big drouth, they put it on the Ol' Man.—Mind, I'm not sayin' they're right. I'm jes' tellin' you. . . .

DORSET. Forgit it. He'll have a hard time witchin' anybody now, from his bed six feet under his wood pile. I reckon we fixed his witchin' business when we throwed dirt in his face. [*He laughs coarsely.*]

COGSWELL. [*Quaking.*] Fo' God's sake, don't talk that way. [DORSET *laughs at him. Then both are silent and listen to the storm outside.* DORSET *continues ruminative, hardly noticing his companion.*] What do you know 'bout it? [*He rises and goes to the fireplace.*] The Cap'n, the Ol' Man, and the locket girl— all hooked up together! This is a funny worl'. An' after all this time, the Cap'n comes back an' gits him. It must've been a long time, too. I been with him five year now. . . . Five year with that man. . . .

DORSET [*Reflectively, standing with his back to the fire.*] Five year up an' down an' 'round about. Gamblin', that's the Cap'n's line. Smooth an' slick, that's the Cap'n! On river boats he used to fleece 'em right an' left. At the race track in New Orleans—in Memphis . . . five year with him . . . an' . . . an' yet . . . I might 'a' knowd somethin' was up.

COGSWELL. Why'd you know?

DORSET. I been with 'im five year an' this is the first time he's ever . . . [*He pauses.*]

COGSWELL. [*Finishing it.*] Killed? That what you mean?

[DORSET *nods.*]

DORSET. That's what.

COGSWELL. Who is he, anyhow?

DORSET. [*With grim humor.*] You ought t' as'd the Ol' Man. He could've tol' you. [*Leaning toward him confidentially.*] Why, at times, Cogswell I think the Cap'n's crazy. [*He jerks his finger toward* THE CAPTAIN *who is now sitting before the fireplace in the rear room, his back to the two.*] Sometimes he gits out by hisself an' talks—talks, mind you, when there's nobody 'round. I found him that way one time. "Cap'n," I says, "what are you doin'?" "Talkin'," he says short-like, and walks away. He's crazy, or he's a funny way of jokin', I tell you.

COGSWELL. [*Shivering.*] What's keepin' us here now? Why does he stay in this ol' house, Dorset?

Tar Heel, December 13, 1919. North Carolina Collection, University of North Carolina at Chapel Hill

PLAYMAKERS PRODUCE A NEW SERIES OF FALL PLAYS; TONIGHT LAST

"WHO PAYS?", "THE HAG", AND "THE THIRD NIGHT" ARE THE TITLES

THIS IS THIRD OF THE SERIES

The Carolina Playmakers under the direction of Professor Koch will present their first program of original folk plays for this season, in the Play-House in the Chapel Hill School on the evenings of Friday and Saturday, December 12 and 13. All seats will be reserved and will be on sale at the drug stores for both performances.

The plays to be produced were selected at the first Author's Reading with especial view to securing a well balanced program. The plays now being rehearsed are Who Pays?, a tragedy of the mill people, by Minnie Shepherd Sparrow; The Third Night, a play of the supernatural, by Thomas Wolfe; and The Hag, a comedy of Folk Superstition, by Elizabeth Lay. The casts of the plays are:

WHO PAYS?

Benson, leader of the striking workers, David R. Hodgin.

Jimmie, his little boy, Clarence Riddle.

Megsie, his little girl, Margaret Bullitt.

Tate, the owner of the firm, Robert Proctor.

Leonora Tate, his daughter, Lina Pruden.

Mrs. Cherrie, a wife of one of the workmen, Eleanor McCarthy.

Mrs. Briggs, another mill woman, Rachel Freeman.

The Doctor, George D. Crawford.

THE THIRD NIGHT

The Cap'n, Thomas Wolfe.

Dorset, Jonathan Daniels.

Cogswell, Fred Cohn.

THE HAG

Sal, a country woman, Mildred Sherrill.

Charlie and Glen, her two little boys, George Winston and Dick Battle.

Mammy, her old mother-in-law, Aline Hughes.

Granny Batts, the old hag, Elizabeth Hughes.

Much interest was shown in the try outs for these plays and since the casts have been made rehearsals have been held each day. In the time left the work has necessarily been concentrated into a short period. The Producing Committee has been divided among the different plays, Dougald MacMillan and Miss Q E directing The Third Night; Minnie Shepherd Sparrow and Cornelia Love, Who Pays? and Elizabeth Lay and Mrs. Weaver The Hag. Professor Koch has general direction of all the plays.

One of the most noticeable features of this co-operaitve play-making is the work of the committees on stage settings and construction and other branches of stage craft. To those who see the plays the general impression is that of a performance worked out thoroughly in all its details. It is a great merit of the organization that this general effect is gained not through individuals but through groups working for the success of the whole performance. So now the stage properties and settings are being collected and the lighting effects arranged. The Carolina Playmakers aim to give an opportunity for creative expression to every member of the community who is interested in the work and thus make the Play-House a truly democratic center of co-operative arts.

The work of the Carolina Playmakers has attracted attention from magazines and papers all over the country. The program to be presented December 12 and 13 will add three new types of folk plays to those produced already and will be only the first of several programs to be presented this year.

DORSET. He's all right. Waitin' till the Asheville stage comes by tomorrow. —Just comes twice a week, don't it?

COGSWELL. [*Eagerly.*] Do we leave tomorrow then?

DORSET. I reckon. [*Ruminating.*] I wonder how the Cap'n 'll split! I wonder what our share will be?

[*As if in answer to the question* THE CAPTAIN *now enters the room. They stare at him, almost in awe.*]

THE CAPTAIN. [*In a cold, severe tone, looking at neither of them.*] We leave here tomorrow morning.—We will divide the money now.

COGSWELL. [*Cringing, yet eager.*] Cap'n, [THE CAPTAIN *does not look at him.*] . . . now, can't we go *now* . . . tonight!

THE CAPTAIN [*Sharply.*] That would be foolish, in this storm. Besides— [*For the first time* THE CAPTAIN *observes* COGSWELL'S *twitching face.*] Eh! Do you wish to go now, Cogswell?

COGSWELL. [*Almost tearfully.*] Yes . . . damn it, I do!

THE CAPTAIN. Very well. Lift the stone, Cogswell.

[THE CAPTAIN *goes to the window and gazes out at the storm, indifferent to the division of the money.* COGSWELL *drops eagerly to his knees and lifts the hearthstone, looking nervously at the blood stains on it. An iron money box fits neatly into the cavity below.* COGSWELL *lifts the lid easily. The box is filled with coins and paper money, the* OLD MAN'S *hoard.* COGSWELL *gives a long exultant sigh as he leans forward, half raising his arm.* DORSET, *looking at the gleaming mass, bends swiftly forward. His eyes glitter. Outside the storm is still raging.*]

COGSWELL. [*After a moment.*] Cap'n . . . for us two, about how much?

THE CAPTAIN. [*Speaking carelessly, over his shoulder.*] As much as you like.

[*The two men, dazed at their good fortune, gaze stupified at each other. Then with a gloating laugh,* COGSWELL *delves both hands into the box, letting the coins ripple through his fingers.*]

[*Suddenly there is a blinding flash of lightning, followed by a roll of thunder which increases in volume until it fills the room. Out of the thunder comes a low, throaty chuckle.* THE CAPTAIN *recoils. In a moment the sound passes.* COGSWELL *is paralyzed. Dorset passes a hand before his eyes. He forces a grim smile.*]

COGSWELL. God help us all . . . the laugh . . . the Ol' Man's laugh!

DORSET. [*Evasively.*] It was the thunder.

COGSWELL. You fool!

THE CAPTAIN. [*Ironically, cold.*] Why don't you take your share, Cogswell?

COGSWELL. [*Whimpering.*] I'll have none of it, I swear I won't!

[*The room has darkened but* COGSWELL *and* DORSET *are vividly silhouetted in the hearth glow.* THE CAPTAIN *stands in semidarkness near the window. He is very erect.*]

DORSET. [*Staring at* THE CAPTAIN—*dully and slowly.*] Let's leave it, Cap'n, let's leave it be.

COGSWELL. [*Whining, rubbing his hands pitifully.*] Yes, yes, Cap'n . . . Let's leave it be, let's leave it be. . . . The Ol' Man'll git us! I tell you he will, Cap'n.

[THE CAPTAIN *laughs sharply. There is a brilliant flash of lightning, followed by a loud peal of thunder which converges in the room.* THE CAPTAIN *walks slowly over to the hearth and faces the door. He appears not agitated, but resolved. The men kneeling on the hearth are stupified.* COGSWELL *is beginning to whimper with fear.* THE CAPTAIN *does not notice them. He opens his shirt bosom and rips from its chain a locket which he wears around his neck. Then laughs harshly.*]

THE CAPTAIN. [*Very softly.*] Journey's end.

[*He hurls the locket into the ashes and re-buttons his shirt. He stands waiting with an intense, listening attitude. The two men stare up at him with open mouths. The wind and rain are heard beating violently against the old house. The door at the left blows open and the rain drives into the room.* THE CAPTAIN *bends forward, losing his composure a little. He speaks with repressed emotion.*]

THE CAPTAIN. All right! What is it . . . what is it, I say? What do you want?

[*He crosses the room slowly, moving toward the door. A vivid flash of lightning which sustains itself for some time makes him turn instinctively toward the window. Dimly outlined through the misted window pane, appears the face of the ghostly* OLD MAN—*even as they killed him. From beneath his red flannel nightcap long stringy white locks may be seen, and in his throat a small bluish hole from* THE CAPTAIN'S *gun. He is looking at* THE CAPTAIN *and chuckling, a horrible soundless chuckle now. But, as the light disappears and the thunder rolls again, it swells to the awful throaty chuckle converging gradually until it fills the entire room, then dies away slowly in the storm.* THE CAPTAIN *is leaning intently toward the window, fascinated. He regains his composure and his dignity quickly, however, and stands facing the spectre in the window. The figure passes slowly by—around the house.*]

THE CAPTAIN. [*Very proud and straight, strides resolutely out of the room.*] I am coming . . . now. . . .

[*The thunder rolls. There is another flash and it converges in the room—the triumphant laugh of the* OLD MAN! COGSWELL *whimpers softly on the hearth.* DORSET *is silent. The ghostly chuckle recedes and is heard faintly in the distance as*

THE CURTAINS CLOSE

The Seniors Say—

Best All 'Round	"WOOLLEY" WHITE
Best Student	"SON" EVERETT
Most Popular	JOHN WASHBURN
Best Athlete	"TODDY" SPAUGH
Best Writer	"TOM" WOLFE
Best Business Man	"BEN" CONE
Best Debater	"BOB" GWYNN
Most Energetic	HENRY STEVENS
Most Dignified	"BILL" BLOUNT
Handsomest	"STAN" TRAVIS
Ugliest	"OTTO" BRYANT
Laziest	"LUKE" UMSTEAD
Best Egg	JOHN WASHBURN
Biggest Politician	"G. D." CRAWFORD
Most Original	"TOM" WOLFE
Prettiest Co-ed	MISS VERA PRITCHARD
Best Dancer	"BILL" NEAL
Wittiest	"TOM" WOLFE
Best Orator	"TROTSKY" MOBLEY

Senior class poll. From *Yackety Yack,* 1920. North Carolina Collection, University of North Carolina at Chapel Hill

"A Previously Unpublished Statement by Thomas Wolfe," 1919

Carolina Quarterly 11 (Spring 1960)

First published in a 1960 *Carolina Quarterly* with an introduction by Frank Kearns, Wolfe's statement was written in 1919 as a class assignment for Professor Frederick Koch's playwriting course.

A.P.M.

A Previously Unpublished Statement by Thomas Wolfe

A Biographical Statement

My writing has undoubtedly been influenced by the work of Mr. George Bernard Shaw, of whom I am an ardent admirer. Of course, there is not the slightest suggestion of the satiric element in either of the two little playlets I have just written. But, nevertheless, in the style, in the rather elaborate explanations of the type of characters, in the extraordinary freedom with which the author's personal views and opinions are expressed in the directions,—in all these I see now the influence of Shaw.

This characteristic of my writings has become evident to me only at this time when, after their completion, I can give them that searching analysis that is made possible by retrospect.

When I see the influence Mr. Shaw has unconsciously exerted on me it is but natural that I should analyze his plays also to find "the reason why." And I have reached this conclusion: Shaw's satirical writing has not influenced me, only so far as their brilliant, scintillating wit have compelled my admiration.

By no stretch of the imagination could I picture myself as a satirist. Indeed, I started my modest career as a "play-maker" by attempting a satiric comedy. It was a false start. It was a dismal failure.

No, it is not the Irishman's satire that interested me, but his prefatory remarks to his plays. To me, Bernard Shaw's prefaces are the most wonderful things he has written. They are far superior to his plays. Why? I believe it is because of the absolute sincerity of his expression of views, and because of the strong, *direct* indignation he manifests in regard to social abuses of the

times. Perhaps, also, personal experiences of the last three months have inclined me more and more to straight-forward, clear-cut absolutely serious
writing.

But it seems to me that in a time of world-woe—woe that has assumed
the proportions of a cataclysm,—we have no place for the witty, but indirect
method of satiric writing. As has been remarked in an article along this line,
the world of today has no ears for the "tiny clap of the doll's house door"—
a noise which satirists over fondly thought was heard around the world. No!
What we need to remedy these existing evils is not writing of this type. We
need (and I will again quote) "the blazing indignation, the thundertones of
a Carlyle—or an Isaiah!" In other words, satire has its province, but it cannot cope with the problems that vitally and immediately face mankind. To
substantiate this, I point to the paucity of successful satire written during the
world war, and to the additional fact that absolutely no writing of this type
has been produced which can combat effectively the cataclysmic evils that
have endangered the world's freedom.

So blind were pre-war satirists, so foolish in their wisdom, that one young
British satirist remarked that there were but two themes left to the modern
reform writer—'Money and Sex.' Today we laugh at his statement as that of
a precocious but misguided youth.

What has all this to do with these two playlets of mine? On the face of
it, nothing. I may remark here, however, that in these playlets I have written
about types of people who [sic] I have known and concerning those I feel
qualified to write about. Of course, I do not preach, nor do I teach, perhaps.
There are no "thunder tones," or "blazing indignation" in them. Yet, they
have suggested a train of thought that intensely interests me and is, I believe,
of vital importance to me. My writing, I feel sure, has been made easier and
better by their production.

And if they have affected my writing to this extent,—if they have indi-
rectly caused an analysis of my writing and a determination of my future
course,—are they not worth while, even tho they be but the amateurish productions of a youngster, at the best?

I hope that you, who may read this, will pardon the divergence from my
prescribed subject, that you will see the connection with the original theme,
and that what I have said will give you new "food for thought" whether you
agree with me in whole, in part, or not at all.

THOMAS WOLFE.

"The Man Who Lives with His Idea," 1920

*Carolina Play-Book of the Carolina Playmakers and the
Carolina Dramatic Association* 16 (March–June 1943): 15–22

The "man" of the title is Frederick H. Koch, and the "idea" is Koch's concept of the folk play. Wolfe takes considerable pains to describe the genesis of the genre as well as Koch's role in the development of the folk-drama movement, first at the University of North Dakota and then at the University of North Carolina.

A.P.M.

The Man Who Lives with His Idea

Which Tells the Story of Frederick H. Koch and
The Playmakers of Chapel Hill

BY THOMAS WOLFE

This article, in manuscript, hitherto unpublished, was written by Thomas Wolfe in the spring of 1920, the year of his graduation from the University of North Carolina. It was discovered by his mother, Julia E. Wolfe, among his literary remains. The last page of the manuscript, now posthumously published, is missing.

Is a successful man full of ideas? Or is his success due to the zeal with which he has carried out the Big Idea? Maybe there are many little ideas which help the big one along. This is the story of a man with one big idea, and how he is putting it across. Fifteen years ago,[1] at the newly established University of North Dakota, a young school growing up out of the level prairie, but filled with the virile spirit of the West, a young Harvard graduate established his residence. His official title in the university catalogue was "Professor of Dramatic Literature." The young professor keenly felt the decadent spirit of the modern stage, which depended to a great degree on risqué sex appeals and shallow plots for its productions.

The folk-lore of the great Northwest country in which the professor, Frederick H. Koch, had settled was new, but it dealt with a pioneer spirit and

---

1. This article was written at Chapel Hill in the Spring of 1920.

the making of a nation. He saw its possibilities. Then the big idea came to him. It was not a new idea, but one as old as civilization—the idea of the folk play, written from character types known in person to the author and from scenes familiar to the writer's own experience.

In the folk play Mr. Koch saw the regeneration of the degenerate modern stage. The educative form of real drama, the drama of the people, became a religion to him. All real drama, he told his pioneer class of playwrights, had to come from the soil. "Get busy and write," he told them, "but write about people and plots that have come within your own experience." Mr. Koch still likes to tell, as illustrative of a wrong conception common to undergraduates today, the story of a sophomore in one of his early composition courses. When asked to hand in a descriptive theme, the student turned in a lurid description of a windstorm raging around the Flatiron building in New York City. "Have you ever been to New York?," Mr. Koch asked the boy. "No, sir," replied the young fellow; and it developed that he had never been out of his native state.

"Then," said Mr. Koch with great emphasis, "why do you write of a windstorm in New York where you have never been, when you have seen *cyclones* in North Dakota?"

"The illustration," says Mr. Koch, "is indicative of the reef on which so many young writers come to grief. The remote scenes of which they have heard divert their energy and their talent from the fairyland at home." Incidentally, the whole episode is indicative of Mr. Koch's method and conception in guiding his young crew of writers.

Mr. Koch was in North Dakota for twelve years. At the State University he organized the Dakota Playmakers and produced the plays written by his classes. His idea made good from the start. In a few years the plays were making an annual tour of the state and had become known to the people throughout the Northwestern territory. The scenes for the plays had been painted by members of the organization, the properties had been constructed or collected by the Playmakers, the whole work of production, in fact, was as good as its name—made and directed by the organization.

The movement was being looked upon as one of national significance, leading national weeklies and theatrical journals began to speak of the "interesting experiment in folk-playmaking that is being carried on in North Dakota." The Dakota Playmakers found time at intervals during the college year, to produce selected plays of modern drama such as Bernard Shaw's *The Devil's Disciple*; or a program of Lady Gregory's Irish folk plays. The college community was being treated to a new program of plays given at a month's frequency throughout the year.

Throughout the state the work on the campus was beginning to have the effect that Mr. Koch had hoped for. To Mr. Koch the campus is but the laboratory testing plant for his idea and he gauges the success of what he sometimes calls his "experiment in folk democracy" by the reception given "the idea" among the people. When, in 1916, the students on the North Dakota campus wrote their own Shakespearean pageant,[2] on the occasion of the Shakespearean tercentenary, and produced it at the university, communities throughout the whole section took up the program and not only produced but wrote their own pageants.

For the first time, perhaps, in American history, we have an illustration of community folk drama. A North Dakota community of only five hundred inhabitants produced its own patriotic masque, *The New Day*.[3] Three hundred people came from all parts of the county—ten, twenty, and thirty miles to rehearsals. Over twenty citizens of the little Dakota village collaborated in writing the pageant which was subsequently published in pamphlet form. Mr. Koch was beginning to see the idea he had lived and put into use come into its own. The collaborative drama that was being produced was the direct result of the work he had started at the university.

The invitation he received in 1917 from the manager of the Washington Square Players of New York City to bring the Dakota Playmakers to New York and give a program of folk plays caused no surprise, for by this time their work had become known throughout the theatrical profession, and several dramatic critics had pointed to the "Dakota idea" as the eventual salvation of the drama. Mr. Koch refused the invitation to go to New York, feeling that for the present the greatest success of the Playmakers was at home. New York, as he said, was not educated to the idea as yet, but that they would eventually receive it was evident.

In 1918, after twelve years residence at the University of North Dakota, Mr. Koch was invited to come to the University of North Carolina, to carry on the work he had established in North Dakota. He accepted. He had seen the "Dakota idea" become a movement, a movement that, after twelve years, was able to continue under its own power and without his further direction.

2. *Shakespeare, the Playmaker,* a Tercentenary Masque, written in collaboration by twenty undergraduate students under the direction of Professor Frederick H. Koch of the Department of Dramatic Literature. (Grand Forks, N. Dak., The University of North Dakota, 1916.) Illustrated.

3. *The New Day,* a Masque of the Future, by Margaret Plank Ganssle, Dakota Playmaker of St. Thomas, N. Dak. (Grand Forks, N. Dak., The Grand Forks Herald Co., 1918.)

Mr. Koch in deciding to come to North Carolina, to the oldest of the state universities, knew that he was making a transition from the new and robust civilization of a newly inhabited country to one of the oldest and most conservative of the states, a state whose leisurely mode of living was entirely different from the hair-trigger action of the Northwest.

"Why did I come?," he says. "In a sense I felt that my work in North Dakota was completed. Why, they're getting along right now in the work just as well as when I was there! North Carolina, to my mind, is a pioneer state, just as much a pioneer state as North Dakota or any of these new Western states. Perhaps it is more of a pioneer state than any of them. Why? It's greatest development is yet to come. It's old, that's so, but its great wealth of natural resources has been almost untouched. And the wealth of folk material here for my work! No state in the country, I believe, offers the wealth of folk-lore and the tradition that North Carolina has to offer. And practically none of this material has been touched."

When Mr. Koch came to Chapel Hill in the fall of 1918 the university had just turned over its plant to the government for the purpose of training officer-material in the Students Army Training Corps. Every normal activity of campus life had been superceded by the military regime, overnight dormitories were labelled with the unfamiliar title of barracks, the university had given itself over wholly and earnestly to the purposes of the government.

Circumstances such as these did not augur well for the beginning of a new group, but shortly after the fall registration Mr. Koch commenced the building of the new organization. A class of fourteen students was already at work writing one-act plays from themes drawn from their own experiences. This little class formed the nucleus of the organization. It is noteworthy that eight members, or over half of the class, were women students. This is remarkable at a state university where the great and inevitable influx of the indomitable "coed" has not yet occurred. Out of a student enrollment of 1200, of which only twenty-five were women students, over one half of Mr. Koch's first class were "coeds." Of course the vast majority of the student body had enlisted for service in the Students Army Training Corps, and were held to a prescribed course training them for military duty. In the classroom work was proceeding rapidly. There were no text books on "The Art of Writing Plays," but a brief survey by Mr. Koch of the fundamental meaning of the folk drama, of the educative force it had displayed in the shaping of civilization, and an account of the work that had been started in North Dakota. Photographs of players and scenes from plays that had been written by North Dakota students were also shown.

One week after the term started he told his class, "I can't tell you how to write a play. There's only one real way. Go ahead and write it. You know enough now to get started. And starting is the hardest part of the game. I can only advise you now to draw up a synopsis of your plot and your story and wade right in. Go on through to the end without stopping, if possible. Then go back, condense, expand, revise as much as is necessary. Then bring it before the class and read it."

When a student completes a play in Mr. Koch's course it is subjected to the "round-table criticism," in which all the members of the class take part. The class is seated around a large table, every effort being made to give an informal atmosphere to the class meetings. The play is read by the author and is then criticized by each member of the class. Mr. Koch puts great dependence in the opinion of the students in the discussions, and the revisions that are made in the play after it is first read to the class are usually the direct result of student criticism. "I find the student to be the best critic in the long run," he says. "It is true they know little of dramatic technique as 'it is done' today, but on the other hand they are not hide-bound by form and their criticisms are usually real and just."

About two dozen plays were written before Christmas in 1918 by Mr. Koch's first class. Three of these were selected finally for production after an "author's reading" had been held which was open to the attendance of the student body. The author's reading, another feature of the Playmakers' method, was attended by a large number of students and they voted by ballot for the three plays that, in their opinion, would give the best program. Mr. Koch had taken the first step, before Christmas, in the organization which was to be known as "The Carolina Playmakers."

The Playmakers, he stated, would bring forth a novel idea in the way of an organization. The restrictions and requirements applying to the usual organization would be practically eliminated. A student, or a member of the university community, automatically became a member of the Playmakers' organization when he rendered the Playmakers a service. There would be no limit to the membership, and any resident of Chapel Hill might be a member. "The Playmakers," however, was well defined and, at the outset, certain committees were appointed to direct the work of the first program of plays. There was a committee on Production selected from faculty and students; a committee on Properties, mainly faculty; a committee on Lighting, composed of the faculty and students from the Department of Electrical Engineering; a committee on Scene Painting, etc. In the meanwhile Mr. Koch was casting the plays. Tryouts had been announced and over fifty candidates for parts responded. A surprising number of candidates showed marked ability and Mr. Koch and his judging committee were correspondingly elated. When the selection of the cast was announced, the unsuccessful candidates were informed that they were regarded as a reserve force and would probably be used in forthcoming productions. These people immediately turned to the aid of the various committees, working with an enthusiasm characteristic of the interest the Playmakers had stirred up on the campus. People from all branches of the life of the university community were working together, the staid professor by his student, the faculty wife by the "coed."

Five months after Mr. Koch's first class met, the first program of folk plays was produced in the auditorium of the schoolhouse at Chapel Hill.[4] The scenes, the properties, the lighting effects, everything that made up the work of production in fact, were home-made—with the exception of the wigs. The plays were given on two consecutive nights and the auditorium, which seats about 600, was filled on both occasions. The school auditorium, since that time the home of Playmaker productions, was christened "The Play-House."

The reaction of the student body and the community to the plays was immediate and enthusiastic. Work was immediately started at once on the production of a second program which, composed of two new plays, was given in May.[5] At Commencement a program of two plays[6] selected from the first two series was given to the visitors. News of the work at Chapel Hill was carried throughout the state, and offers began to pour in on Mr. Koch to bring his plays to various towns in the state.

National recognition was being given the "experiment." *The Baltimore Sun*[7] carried a feature story in a Sunday edition, several New York papers

4. The first program of "Carolina Folk Plays," March 14 and 15, 1919, staged on the newly-improvised stage in the auditorium of the Chapel Hill High School Building. The plays were: *When Witches Ride,* a play of Carolina folk superstition, by Elizabeth A. Lay, *The Return of Buck Gavin,* a tragedy of the mountain people, by Thomas Wolfe, *What Will Barbara Say?*, a romance of Chapel Hill, by Minnie Shepherd Sparrow.

5. The second bill of "Carolina Folk Plays," May 30 and 31, 1919: *The Fighting Corporal,* a comedy of Negro life, by Louisa Reid, *Peggy,* a tragedy of the tenant farmer, by Harold Williamson.

6. The first Commencement production of The Carolina Playmakers, June 17, 1919: *What Will Barbara Say?*, a romance of Chapel Hill, by Minnie Shepherd Sparrow; *Peggy,* a tragedy of the tenant farmer, by Harold Williamson.

7. Evidently Tom Wolfe was referring here to the feature story "University of North Carolina is Presenting Made-In-America Plays" published in *The Globe,* Boston, Mass., April 13, 1919. The story is illustrated with a photograph of Tom as Buck Gavin

editorialized on the work. In September the *Review of Reviews*[8] published an article of the work that had been done together with pictures of the first three plays, *When Witches Ride,* a play of folk superstition among the natives of Eastern North Carolina; *The Return of Buck Gavin,* a tragedy of the mountain people in Western Carolina; and *What Will Barbara Say?,* a romance of Chapel Hill. The editor of the *American Review of Reviews* closed his article with the following significant statement: "Their efforts . . . deserve commendation from every man and woman who has our country's welfare at heart. . . . When every community has its Playhouse and its own native group of plays and producers we shall have a national American theatre that will give a richly varied authentic expression of American life."

Since last spring the work of The Carolina Playmakers has gone steadily ahead. Shortly before Christmas the third series[9] of plays was produced and the reception given them demonstrated that the work of the Playmakers had lost none of its interest to the students. By way of variety the Playmakers produced in March Oscar Wilde's three act comedy *The Importance of Being Earnest,*[10] and the work of the players showed an exceptionally polished technique.

The fourth series[11] of plays has just been produced. The first trip of the Playmakers, taking their wares to the people has just been made. On Friday, May 7, the latest program was given to the people of Greensboro.[12] The new Municipal Theatre in that town was well-filled and the *Greensboro News* next morning stated conservatively the opinion of the townspeople when it said, "The plays were marked by an exceptional order of dramatic talent."

---

in his first play, *The Return of Buck Gavin,* and two scenes from Elizabeth Lay's *When Witches Ride.*

8. "The Carolina Playmakers," editorial article by Dr. Albert Shaw. *The American Review of Reviews,* September 1919. Illustrated.

9. The third bill of "Carolina Folk Plays," December 12 and 13, 1919: *Who Pays,* a tragedy of industrial conflict, by Minnie Shepherd Sparrow; *The Third Night,* a mountain play of the supernatural, by Thomas Wolfe; *The Hag,* a comedy of folk-superstition, by Elizabeth A. Lay.

10. March 1 and 2, 1920.

11. The fourth bill of "Carolina Folk Plays," April 30 and May 1, 1920: *The Bell Buoy,* a tragedy of the North Carolina coast, by Dougald MacMillan; *The Last of the Lowries,* a play of the Robeson County outlaws, by Paul Green. *"Dod Gast Ye Both!,"* a comedy of mountain moonshiners, by Hubert Heffner.

12. *Ibid.* May 7, 1920. This was the first showing of "Carolina Folk Plays" outside of Chapel Hill.

THE CAROLINA PLAY-BOOK

now for the extension of the work so well begun, to see it spread in time to every hamlet in the state, and to go beyond. He dreams of the day when every township will have its own community theatre, and when that theatre will be the workshop for people who will literally be making their own plays out of their own lives, will all be Playmakers.

Mr. Koch illustrates every day the fact that he and his "Idea" are inseparable. If you visit him at his home he will be "talking shop" to you before he knows it, but to talk shop with a man who believes in his wares to the consuming extent that Mr. Koch does, is a very lively and interesting conversation. He becomes indignant if he hears the individual Playmakers classified as amateurs or the work of the Playmakers as an amateur production. "We're not amateurs," he says, "in the sense that our work is amateurish. We have nothing in common with . . .

The Man Who Lives With His Idea[1]

Which Tells The Story of Frederick H Koch And The Playmakers of Chapel Hill

Is a successful man "full of ideas"? Or is his success due to the zeal with which he has carried out the 'Big Idea?' Maybe there are many little ideas which help the big one along.

This is the story of a man with one big idea, and how he is putting it across.

Facsimile of the beginning of the above manuscript.

22

The last page from Wolfe's article, with a facsimile of his handwriting. *Carolina Play-Book,* March 1943

Are the students at Chapel Hill writing any plays that are really worth while? Perhaps the comment of Professor Manly, head of the English Department at the University of Chicago, and a distinguished authority on the drama, will answer the question. Several of the plays, which are going to be included in the Playmakers' first book, were sent to Professor Manly for editing and possible changes in dialogue. After he had finished editing *Peggy,* a one-act play dealing with the life of the tenant farmer in North Carolina, Mr. Manly penciled in the margin the following: "There are flashes of dialog in this play that remind me of Synge's best style." Incidentally a firm of theatrical producers is considering *Peggy* with a view toward production.

Mr. Koch feels that the time for classing the work in Dakota and North Carolina as an "interesting experiment" has passed. The work and the results of the Playmakers organization is proof of its own success. He looks now for the extension of the work so well begun, to see it spread in time to every hamlet in the state, and to go beyond. He dreams of the day when every township will have its own community theatre, and when that theatre will be the workshop for people who will literally be making their own plays out of their own lives, will all be Playmakers.

Mr. Koch illustrates every day the fact that he and his "Idea" are inseparable. If you visit him at his home he will be "talking shop" to you before he knows it, but to talk shop with a man who believes in his wares to the consuming extent that Mr. Koch does, is a very lively and interesting conversation. He becomes indignant if he hears the individual Playmakers classified as amateurs or the work of the Playmakers as an amateur production. "We're not amateurs," he says, "in the sense that our work is amateurish. We have nothing in common with . . .

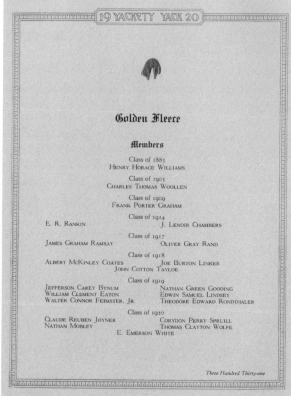

Election to the Golden Fleece society was the highest undergraduate honor at the University of North Carolina. Wolfe is standing at the center in the photo. From *Yackety Yack,* 1920. North Carolina Collection, University of North Carolina at Chapel Hill

ATTRIBUTIONS

Thomas Wolfe has been credited with the authorship of dozens of unsigned contributions to the *Tar Heel* during his junior (1918–19) and senior (1919–20) years at the University of North Carolina, when he was managing editor and editor-in-chief of the UNC student newspaper. These attributions are plausible but unsupported by evidence, apart from anecdotage: that Wolfe wrote all of the editorials during his tenure as editor-in-chief and that he wrote entire issues of campus publications. These claims are appropriate to the legendary aspects of Wolfe's undergraduate career, but they are not reliable.

There are three sources for most of the attributions: Agatha Boyd Adams, "Thomas Wolfe at Chapel Hill," *Carolina Quarterly* 2 (December 1949): 21–40 (untrustworthy; lacks evidence as well as dates and correct titles); Adams, *Thomas Wolfe: Carolina Student* (Chapel Hill: University of North Carolina Library, 1950) (untrustworthy and undocumented); and Richard Walser, *Thomas Wolfe Undergraduate* (Durham, N.C.: Duke University Press, 1977). Walser is the best of the three, but it apparently relies on Adams. Walser's attributions are supported by the correspondence of Wolfe's schoolmates.

The three major Wolfe biographies provide inadequate or undocumented data on his University of North Carolina publications. Elizabeth Nowell, *Thomas Wolfe* (Garden City, N.Y.: Doubleday, 1960) relied on Don Bishop's "Tom Wolfe as Student," *Carolina Magazine* (March 1942). Andrew Turnbull, *Thomas Wolfe* (New York: Scribners, 1967) made no effort to identify or evaluate Wolfe's college writings. David Herbert Donald, *Look Homeward: A Life of Thomas Wolfe* (Boston: Little, Brown, 1987) borrowed from Walser without verifying his borrowings. Thus: "He started, for instance, a series called 'Fable of Sultan Peikh A Bou.'" Nowell was not a trained scholar; Donald and Turnbull received doctorates in history from Harvard.

This volume reprints four *Tar Heel* items: three for which a convincing case was made by Walser and one of which was identified by Frederick Koch. The other attributions are listed—with no confidence—for the record. It is a disservice to Thomas Wolfe and serious readers to augment his canon with ghosts.

M.J.B.

Attributions

"Fables of Sultan Peikh A Bou," *Tar Heel,* October 9, 1918, 2; October 16, 1918, 2; February 14, 1919, 3. Attributed to Wolfe by Donald, 51; no source provided.

"Solons Gather Around the Festive Board in a Joyous Love-Feast . . . but Bolshevist Runs Amuck," *Tar Heel,* March 28, 1919, 1, 3. Remotely possible that this is unidentified article on bolshevism in colleges listed by Adams.

"A Carolina Man," *Tar Heel,* October 11, 1919, 2. Identified by Adams as "What Constitutes a Carolina Man?" See Walser, 105.

"Clean Sportsmanship," *Tar Heel,* October 25, 1919, 2. Editorial attributed to Wolfe by Adams.

"Deserves Support," *Tar Heel,* November 1, 1919, 2. See Walser, 105.

* "Tar Heels Despite Defeat of Last Week Await Virginians," *Tar Heel,* November 15, 1919, 1, 3.

"A Welcome to Our Visitors," *Tar Heel,* November 27, 1919, 2. See Walser, 107.

"The Sweetest Story Ever Told; N.C., 6–Va., 0," *Tar Heel,* December 6, 1919, 1. See Walser, 107. Also attributed to Wolfe by Adams.

"It Was a Great Game," *Tar Heel,* December 6, 1919, 2. See Walser, 107.

* "Ye Who Have Been There Only Know," *Tar Heel,* December 13, 1919, 2.

"With Apologies to Pepys," *Tar Heel,* January 10, 1920, 2; January 23, 1920, 6; January 30, 1920, 3; February 7, 1920, 3; February 14, 1920, 4; February 21, 1920, 4; February 28, 1920, 3; March 13, 1920, 3; April 2, 1920, 4; May 8, 1920, 3; May 22, 1920, 4. Attributed to Wolfe by Nowell, 38, and Turnbull, 36; no evidence provided.

Untitled editorial: "During the week . . . ," *Tar Heel,* January 30, 1920, 2. See Walser, 113. Identified by Adams as "The Danger of Snow Balls."

"Nor Shall We Loaf Hereafter," *Tar Heel,* February 7, 1920, 2. See Walser, 113. Identified by Adams as "Clean Up Week."

"Doings of a Carolina Man," *Tar Heel,* February 14, 1920, 6. See Walser, 113.

* "Useful Advice to Candidates," *Tar Heel,* February 28, 1920, 2.

"To the Student Body," *Tar Heel,* February 28, 1920, 2. Identified by Adams as "Crowded Conditions in Class Rooms and Dormitories."

"The Tar Heel: State Ticket for Governor," *Tar Heel,* February 28, 1920, 1. See Walser, 115.

* "The Bibiograph," *Tar Heel,* March 13, 1920, 2.

* Unsigned attribution reprinted here.

"This Is No Place for a Thief," *Tar Heel,* March 13, 1920, 2. See Walser, 113.

"The Tapping of the Golden Fleece," *Tar Heel,* April 2, 1920, 2. See Walser, 113.

Tar Baby, April 10, 1920. This issue is a parody of the *Raleigh News and Observer.* Thomas C. Wolfe is identified on the masthead as "Editor of this issue." The myth-making biographical process has credited him with authorship of the "entire issue" (Turnbull)—or at least most of it. Since there are no bylines, it is impossible to identify Wolfe's contributions. See Don Bishop, "Tom Wolfe as a Student," *Carolina Magazine,* March 1942; reprinted in *The Enigma of Thomas Wolfe,* edited by Richard Walser (Cambridge: Harvard University Press, 1953), 8–17:

> On one occasion he was designated by the editor of the *Tar Baby,* the humor magazine, to be guest editor of the publication for one issue. The regular editor hounded Wolfe, but on the day the material must be in the hands of the printer, he had still turned in nothing. The editor cornered Wolfe and demanded action. So he sat down after supper and wrote the issue from cover to cover, forty-five pages of satire modeled after one of the newspapers of the state.

This is a good scuttlebutt anecdote, but there is no supporting evidence.

"Athletic Courtesy and Lack of It," *Tar Heel,* April 24, 1920, 2. See Walser, 113. Also attributed to Wolfe by Adams.

"The Parson and His Workshop," *Tar Heel,* May 8, 1920, 2. See Walser, 113.

"She Deserved a Bigger Crowd," *Tar Heel,* May 15, 1920, 2. See Walser, 113.

"Di Society Favors Anthony Amendment," *Tar Heel,* May 22, 1920, 6. Identified by Adams as "Women Suffrage."

"Graves Says It Flows Freely in N. Carolina," *Tar Heel,* May 29, 1920, 1. Identified by Adams as "Many Moonshiners in Orange County."

"A Remedy for Midnight," *Tar Heel,* May 29, 1920, 2. See Walser, 115.

"On Finishing Our Job," *Tar Heel,* June 5, 1920, 2. Editorial attributed to Wolfe by Adams.

Wolfe was the assistant editor-in-chief for the *Magazine* (December 1919–May 1920), in which there are unsigned editorials.

"Tar Heels Despite Defeat of Last Week Await Virginians," 1919

Tar Heel, November 15, 1919, 1, 3

See Albert Coates, "'Memories of Thomas Wolfe' by His Schoolmates," *Thomas Wolfe of North Carolina,* edited by H. G. Jones (Chapel Hill: North Caroliniana Society and North Carolina Collection, 1982), 57–58:

> There was the night before the Carolina-VMI football game in Chapel Hill, while he was editor-in-chief on the *Tar Heel.* He came to my room with this complaint:
>
> > Albert, we have had a sorry team this year, the students have had no enthusiasm for it, and now at the end of the season they are becoming ashamed of themselves, and putting the blame on me and the *Tar Heel* for lack of whipping up the Carolina spirit and supporting the team. I am going out to cover the game tomorrow myself and write the news story, and see that the *Tar Heel* supports the team.
>
> VMI beat Carolina 29 to nothing and Jimmy Leach on the VMI team was the hero of the day. Tom's description of the game was a burst of journalistic satire written in this vein: "Leach ran around Carolina's right end for forty-five yards, only to be downed in his tracks." You will find it in the *Tar Heel* on the day after the game in the fall of 1919.
> —Albert Coates

See also Walser, 105.

M.J.B.

Tar Heels Despite Defeat of Last Week Await Virginians

North Carolina's football machine suffered a bad attack of carburetor rheumatism last Saturday on Emerson Field and V. M. I. won 29–7. The Great God Dope left the field immediately after the game and his bellows of agony could be heard on the campus until 10 o'clock that night, when he died in Battle Park.

The game was replete with thrilling plays and first class football. The trouble was: V. M. I. held the monopoly.

The fast. . . . . and powerful Carolina backfield ripped through the V. M. I. line and tore around the ends with the speed of the agile steam tractor as it leaps nimbly o'er the hillside.

The battle was friendly fought throughout and the size of the score was at all times in doubt. First Mr. Leach, who attends school at V. M. I., would grab the ball and race 40 yards up the field when Carolina's unpregnable defence would stiffen and throw him for a loss. Then Mr. Leach would go around end for 15 yards only to run against the same obstacle as before.

Before defense such as this V. M. I. was helpless and was held to a baggardly 29 points.

Seriously, however, the game was a bitter pill, but such doses are often needed. We need our overconfidence well cleaned out. And the game was the best thing that could have happened to our student body and our team.

To be beaten by a team which in its turn has been swamped the week before by N. C. State, an eleven we have trounced, is no easy dose. But it happened. And let there be no mistaking this part. The light cadet team had the upper hand at all stages; they played rings all around us. They deserved to win. The only time our boys recovered from their semi-hypnotic trance was at the beginning of the second half when they received the ball and drove straight through the cadet line for five first downs and a score.

The team is not to be blamed. Overconfidence perhaps played a small part in their defeat. What is more likely however is that the mid-season slump which comes to many teams struck us at this period. And it is exceedingly fortunate that it does come now. The first climax of the season was reached October 23 at Raleigh when, after weeks of strained tension we defeated N. C. State in a grueling contest.

The natural tendency was to relax; the team did this.

Making no excuses for our defeat from the splendid cadet eleven, we are still firm in our contention that with the Carolina team playing as it played N. C. State, the cadets would have bit the dust.

But—we look forward now. Defeat will help our team. They are coming out of their slump and on Turkey Day (this is our prediction), we will see the machine at its highest form.

STUDENT BODY HOLDS PEP MEETING AND SNAKE DANCE ON ATHLETIC FIELD

Tar Heel, November 15, 1919; see the third paragraph. North Carolina Collection, University of North Carolina at Chapel Hill

Are we down hearted? H— No', was the answer as expressed by a large majority of the student body that gathered on the tennis courts where a series of yells began and sent their echo to every part of the campus and athletic field, Monday evening at four thirty, following up the suggestion made by Frank Graham, Monday morning in chapel.

The crowd began to gather soon after the ringing of the four-thirty bell, and grew in immensity with each moment. A few minutes after the bell had rung, "pep" and enthusiasm was at its height. No onlooker would ever have dreamed that that enormous crowd of students were cheering a team that had gone down to defeat only two days before. In that mass meeting was exemplified the true spirit of Carolina, a spirit that knows no defeat, and cherishes every victory.

When the crowd had completely gathered the yells began, lead by Tom Wolfe and G. D. Crawford. They were not content to remain out of sight of the team they were so heartily cheering, and as an irresistible wave they swept down on the athletic field, where yells were again given for the team. After many and long lusty yells, they began a snake dance around the field, which is emblamatic of victory and not defeat. And a victory it was for them for the spirit that prevailed knows no defeat. The team, every member of it knows that the student body is behind it to a man.

When the students had yelled to their hearts content, when they were completely satisfied that they had expressed themselves well, they disbursed, each as happy as if a victory had been won.

"Ye Who Have Been There Only Know," 1919

Tar Heel, December 13, 1919, 2

Walser ("An Early Wolfe Essay—and the Downfall of a Hero," *Modern Fiction Studies* 11 [Autumn 1965]: 269–74) discusses connections between "Ye Who Have Been There Only Know" and *The Web and the Rock:* "While it is unsigned, no one can doubt that nineteen-year-old editor Tom Wolfe was the author." See Don Bishop, "Thomas Wolfe's First Fame Came from Essay on Labor," *Durham Morning Herald,* April 20, 1941, 3, 8: "For example, the *Tar Heel* of December 13, 1919 carried this article on the Virginia-Carolina football game of 1917. *It was unsigned but obviously by Wolfe*" (emphasis added). No evidence for this. Also attributed to Wolfe by Adams.

M.J.B.

Ye Who Have Been There Only Know
"On to Richmond!"

Thanksgiving after Thanksgiving daring would rise that challenge, and the day before the game would see an entire student body migrating. Frantic preparations everywhere, pleading letters to dad, wholesale borrowing from everybody. Bonfires and pep and always more pep, with always some wild eyed dervish leading on in split Carolinas. Do you remember how old Henry, and short Bill Jones and Dean Andy used to campaign for weeks to raise capital enough to make the trip on?

When twilight comes, the long train moves slowly out of Carrboro, to University, to Durham and then North the railheads clicking "On to Richmond, On to Richmond, On to Richmond." Somehow there is an air abroad that catches men's enthusiasm. From one end of the train to the other, there is feverish delight. A kind of quivering anticipation for the morrow would prevent one from sleep, coiled up on the red plush seats, even if ambitious fellow travelers would permit it. Some ingenious soul has fabricated a palatial couch, and is just about to sink into sleep when the voice of energy cries in his ear. "On to Richmond" and the arm of enthusiasm dumps him upon the floor of the coach. Dopesters run wild while about them an eager bunch find just how the game is going. Hours of sustained revelry steal away the night and gray morning finds old Richmond stealing by. We come to rest beside the James.

Every man makes his own day. Troop up the streets. Stop at the stands and deck yourself in blue and white. Take your own way, but come at last to the Jefferson and there under the columns yell yourself hoarse in a rapt vindication of the worth of a great football team. Sure we were beaten last year and the year before and . . . but never mind that. Today we win.

March in the wild revolutionary mob to the Park. Crush and crunch yourself into the Broad St. stands and then for an hour and a half forget all these little things of life and living. Somehow your very soul is out there with those eleven men, fighting, fighting in the interest of a cause that you feel to be worthy of any sacrifice.

Was the scene for us or against us? Too often against us. And yet while the bitterness of defeat or the flush of victory is vivid. We know that whatever the result the game was worth while. Strength, cleanness, swiftness, all have been dramatized before us.

Supper, the report of the game, speeches in the Murphy from the lobby table, the Lyric, all pass in swift and dazed before a pair of sleep-blurred eyes. How you ever found your car you do not know, or how you tumbled into a berth or curled up on a seat for that sweet sleep that could come at last when all the shouting and tumult had spent itself.

You come back to the Hill now as you came back then. Once again in your memory let flash the vivid scenes that you will never forget. The touchdown with Bill Folger over the line . . . men chanting victory and dancing in serpentine coils . . . Roy Homewood and his tribe arm and arm through the streets . . . the faculty le-hic-ture at the rear of the homebound car . . . and then with the red dawn of a new college day and a new college generation come back across the campus and with that which thou hast in that heavy ragged suitcase of thine give a toast "To the Days that are Gone."

"Useful Advice to Candidates," 1920

Tar Heel, February 28, 1920, 2

See Walser, *Thomas Wolfe Undergraduate,* 113–15. Also attributed to Wolfe by Adams. Although there is no solid proof for Wolfe's authorship of this editorial, it has been credited to him in the recollections of his college friends.

M.J.B.

Useful Advice to Candidates

Mr. O. Max Gardners' address to the student body on Wednesday night, marks the beginning of a series of addresses to be made here by all the Democratic candidates for Governor, and the Republicans, also, if they can be brought here. Thus does the University step boldly into the arena of impartial politics and gives the pleasant challenge to these gentlemen to come here and show their wares. Not having had time to prepare our invaluable little booklet: "Handbook of Useful Information to those Gubernatorially Inclined, Who Will Speak at Chapel Hill," we beg to herewith append a few admonitions that may be useful to them.

1. Remember that you are speaking to a fair-minded, impartial group of men, who have small respect for petty appeals of a partisan nature.

2. Remember that you will be hospitably and courteously received, whether we approve of you or not. It is therefore your own fault if you don't appear to your best advantage.

3. Tell us something we don't already know. We will agree quite freely that the Old North State is the peer of them all and that the labor situation is serious. But if you will come boldly forward and exhibit two or three planks out of your platform that shows you have been doing some real thinking on your own part, we will have more respect for you, no matter if we don't all agree with you.

4. And remember lastly, gentlemen, that you yourself will be either the vindication or condemnation to your claims for the Governorship. We are interested in you, the man; in the evidences of your own individuality and not in your party politics. You find us with minds open, receptive and unprejudiced; in the one brief hour that is yours before us we'll make our decision about you, and the tag we put upon you is likely to be the right one. Yours with kindness and friendship.—The Student Body.

"The Bibiograph," 1920

Tar Heel, March 13, 1920, 2

See Walser, *Thomas Wolfe Undergraduate,* 155n55: "In Carolina Playmakers Scrapbook (NcU), 1:108, there is a handwritten notation, probably by Koch, that 'Bibliograph' is 'by T.C.W.'"

M.J.B.

The Bibiograph
It is an excellent thing to watch
The work of Frederick Henry Koch
If thou art one who wields the hammer
Upon our present boudoir drammer,
Or if a stage you crave that's better,
A true-folk drama to the letter,
You'll get right here the artist's thrill
The Renaissance of Chapel Hill.
And soon 'neath every roof and steeple
You'll hear the "Drammer of the Peepul."
And if you have the will to act
But live in ignorance to this fact,
An erstwhile unpotential factor
Will be o'ernight a polished actor.
The very crudest hick, in truth,
Becomes straightway a stalwart youth;
Fame, fortune, and the arts come whizzin',
In fact, o'ernight, the world is his'n.
His life set free from boudoir's fetters
His name appears in gilded letters,
And Eubanks windows hastes to say
That "C. McBoob in his own play,
Will present tonight in one brief act act
That polished gem: 'Her Lack of Tact,'
This program being the top notch

Of Director-General Frederick Koch."
Thus doth this man the lowly raise
And carry to fame by writing plays.
It is an excellent thing to say
That thou are "F. K's" protégé.

The Tar Baby, Inc.

Published by the students of the University of North Carolina.

Office, Kluttz Building, Chapel Hill, N. C.

Published throughout the college year, fifteen copies a year.
Subscription price three dollars a year, twenty-five cents the copy.

Entered as second class mail matter at the postoffice at Chapel Hill, N. C.

Board of Editors and Managers

Editor of this issue.........................Thomas C. Wolfe

THE STAFF

Editor-in-Chief.......................Henry D. Stevens
Business Manager...................Ernest H. Abernethy
Managing Editor.......................Legette Blythe
Art Editor...........................Clarence R. Sumner

All contributions should be addressed to the Editor-in-Chief (11 Pettigrew), business communications to the Business Manager (9 Carr), and drawings to the Art Editor (Tar Heel Tavern). The Board reserves the privilege of moderate revision of accepted articles.

Printed by the Seeman Printery, Durham, N. C.

Vol. 1, No. 9   April 10, 1920   New Series

Masthead for the *Tar Baby,* the university humor magazine, 1920. North Carolina Collection, University of North Carolina at Chapel Hill

The President, Professors, and Board of Trustees
of the

University of North Carolina

TO ALL TO WHOM THESE PRESENTS SHALL COME

Greeting:

Whereas it is the ancient right and duty of Universities to reward meritorious attainments in Scholarship, and whereas

Thomas Clayton Wolfe

has honorably fulfilled the requirements imposed by the University, now, therefore, We, under the authority of the Constitution of the State of North Carolina, have with due form admitted him to the degree of **Bachelor of Arts** granting therewith all the rights, honors, and privileges thereunto appertaining.

In witness whereof the Seal of the University and the signatures of the President, Professors, and Board of Trustees are hereunto affixed.

Given at Chapel Hill, in the State of North Carolina, this 16th day of June in the year of Our Lord 1920 and of this University the 125th

Professors:
Thos. J. Wilson, Jr., Registrar.

H. W. Chase, President.
Trustees:

THE UNIVERSITY OF NORTH CAROLINA

NAME Wolfe - Thomas Clayton ENTERED Sep. 1916 COURSE A.B.
NAME OF FATHER W. O. Wolfe P.O. Asheville STATE N.C.
BORN 3 Oct. 1900 PREPARATORY SCHOOL OR COLLEGE North State School.

Wolfe's diploma and the transcript of his college grades. North Carolina Collection, University of North Carolina at Chapel Hill

Appendix A

The Peace Treaty including the Constitution of the League of States Adopted by the English 21 Conference of the University of North Carolina Chapel Hill, March 28, 1919

In the early winter of Thomas Wolfe's junior year, Professor Edwin Greenlaw organized his English 21 class into a peace conference designed to resolve problems facing nations at the end of World War I, with groups of students representing delegations from these nations. According to the foreword to the treaty, "The important issues which affected the various nations were thoroughly investigated by the delegates of the nations interested or by committees from several nations."

In addition to being one of the five representatives for the United States, Wolfe was a member of the Commission on Indemnities and of the Commission on Freedom of the Seas, but he was not listed as a member of the committee responsible for the final draft of the treaty. As managing editor of the *Tar Heel*, he publicized the progress of the Peace Conference. The February 14, 1919, *Tar Heel* reported that the class expected to finish its work "before the constitution drawn up by the Peace Conference in Paris was made public." On the evening of March 24, 1919, the last day of examinations, Wolfe attended a party at Greenlaw's home to celebrate completion of the treaty.

An unsigned article in the April 4, 1919, *Tar Heel*, probably written by Wolfe and titled "Peace Treaty Will Be Published by Conference," reported:

> The Peace Treaty was finally adopted on March 31 by the Peace Conference in English 21, and its publication was authorized. The Treaty includes articles fixing the responsibility for the war, the military and naval terms of peace, the indemnity terms imposed on Germany, definite settlements for territorial disputes and mandatory problems, the position of new states, and articles providing for the establishment of a strong League of States, which go a long way toward preventing future wars.
>
> The Conference believes that in this Treaty it has embodied the right solution for most of the world's big problems. The Treaty is built on facts obtained by extensive and careful investigation. Slavish imitation of the Paris Conference has been avoided. In fact most of the provisions of the constitution were decided upon before the publication of the Paris Conference's

constitution. The Conference hopes that upon the publication of this Treaty the thinking men of the University and the state will give it careful consideration. If the document succeeds in creating a greater interest in the international situation and greater support for the League of Nations, its purpose will have been attained.

Two weeks after this article appeared, the April 18, 1919, *Tar Heel* reported that copies of the twenty-page pamphlet edition of the treaty were selling in great numbers.

The April 4, 1919, *Tar Heel* reported that the *New York Times* had suggested in an editorial that the English 21 Peace Treaty was probably as good as anything that might come out of Versailles. The *Tar Heel* article also reported that the New York Public Library had ordered a copy for its collection. This copy and two others in the North Carolina Collection at the Wilson Library, University of North Carolina at Chapel Hill, have been located by the editors.

A.P.M.

North Carolina Collection, University of North Carolina at Chapel Hill

The Peace Treaty

INCLUDING

The Constitution of the League of States

ADOPTED BY

The English 21 Conference
of the
University of North Carolina

Chapel Hill
March 28, 1919

Foreword

This Peace Treaty and Constitution of the League of States is the product of twelve weeks' work by the class in English 21, a course in English composition for Juniors and Seniors, under the direction of Dr. Edwin Greenlaw, at the University of North Carolina. The class was organized into a Peace Conference, being divided into a number of groups, each acting as the delegation from an important nation. The meetings of the Conference were presided over by officers elected from the class, and were conducted largely according to the ideas of the students themselves. The important issues which affected the various nations were thoroughly investigated by the delegates of the nations interested or by committees from several nations. The results of the investigations were presented to the Conference; and after due discussion and debate each question at issue was settled by the vote of the Conference. The decisions resulting from these investigations and deliberations are embodied in the document that follows.

E. S. LINDSEY,
President of the Conference.

The Organization of the Conference

President—E. S. Lindsey
Secretaries—R. W. Madry, F. G. Miles

REPRESENTATIVES FROM

The United States of America
  J. W. G. Powell, *Chairman*
  T. C. Wolfe
  L. H. Bryant
  J. F. Spainhour, Jr.
  J. L. Aycock
France
  R. B. Gwynn, *Chairman*
  M. Rountree
  H. D. Stevens
  L. G. Travis
Japan
  R. F. Moseley
  ———
Russia
  L. B. Willis, *Chairman*
  W. M. York
  E. E. White
  N. Mobley

Great Britain
  L. H. Hodges, *Chairman*
  F. L. Townsend
  E. S. Merritt
  J. E. Dowd
  T. S. Kittrell
Italy
  W. P. Andrews, *Chairman*
  W. E. Price
  B. C. Jones
  P. F. Lynch
Belgium
  B. Cone, *Chairman*
  E. E. Rives
The Balkan States
  F. G. Miles, *Chairman*
  E. M. Spencer
  J. R. Morris
  W. H. Williamson

Germany
H. G. West

Indemnities		Steering Committee		Constitution	
Wolfe	Morris	York	Price	Gwynn	Price
York	Lynch	Hodges	Gwynn	Mobley	Aycock
Rives	Rountree	Miles		Cone	
Merritt	West				

Final Draft of Peace Treaty		Territorial Adjustments	
Moseley	Bryant	White	Cone
York	Rountree	Mobley	Lynch
Kittrell			

Freedom of the Seas		Mandatories	
Wolfe	Spainhour	Hodges	Dowd
Stevens	Rives	Jones	Powell

The Peace Treaty Including the Constitution of the League of States

Preamble

The representatives of the United States of America, Great Britain, France, Italy, Japan, Belgium, Brazil, China, Cuba, Greece, Guatemala, Hayti, Honduras, Liberia, Panama, Portugal, Rumania, Serbia, Siam, Germany, Austria, Bulgaria, and Turkey, gathered in conference at Chapel Hill, North Carolina, March 28, 1919, for the settlement of the problems of the late war between the Allied Powers and the Central Powers, do hereby agree to the following treaty for the establishment of peace.

The Central Powers, hereinafter referred to as Germany and her Allies, include Germany, Austria, Turkey, and Bulgaria.

Article I

RESPONSIBILITY FOR THE WAR

Section 1. The Government of Germany had for many years been preparing for war, and, having attained the preparation with which victory appeared certain, was only waiting for a favorable opportunity to open hostilities. The Government of Germany seized upon the Austrian difficulty with Serbia as a convenient means for attaining its ends and inspired Austria to make demands on Serbia which she could not grant without surrendering her sovereignty. On July 5, 1914, in a conference at Potsdam, the rulers and military leaders of the German Empire definitely decided on war and took steps to recall from foreign countries German loans, ships, and men.

Sec. 2. The Government of Germany deliberately disregarded all attempts at mediation. It secretly backed Austria in her demands and openly refused to allow compromise. Prince Lichnowsky, at that time German ambassador to England, has stated that the German Government could have prevented war if it had desired, but instead it desired war, and refused to take any steps to prevent it. Germany's hurried mobilization, her immediate attack, her unhesitating violation of the neutrality of Belgium, show a fixed and steady purpose to plunge the world into war.

Sec. 3. In the prosecution of this war, Austria, Turkey, and Bulgaria were allied with Germany; but, since Germany dominated the governments of her allies and used them as tools, the German Government is held primarily responsible for the war.

Sec. 4. In view of these facts, Germany and her allies shall deliver to the Allied High Commission provided for in Article V of this treaty, those persons whom the high commission, or a subcommission to be appointed by it, shall decide to have been primarily responsible for the war and for the illegal and barbarous practices thereof, in order that these persons may be tried and properly punished by a judicial tribunal to be appointed by the Allied High Commission. Germany and her allies shall also co-operate with the aforesaid Allied Commission in securing for trial, and for punishment if convicted, those persons held responsible by the Commission who have already fled or who may hereafter flee to other countries.

Article II

MILITARY AND NAVAL PROVISIONS

Section 1. The military, naval, and air forces and all equipment and instruments of war of Germany and her Allies shall be reduced to such a standard as will render these powers unable to conduct offensive warfare, provided, however, that these powers shall be allowed to maintain military forces, with proper equipment, sufficient to enable them to prevent internal disorders.

Sec. 2. The members of the military forces just provided for shall be volunteers, whose terms of service shall not be less than eight years.

Sec. 3. The naval vessels which have been surrendered by Germany and her Allies to the Allied Powers shall be scrapped and sold, the proceeds being distributed among the Allied Powers in proportion to their losses of shipping tonnage in the war.

Sec. 4. In order that the preceding provisions of this article may be enforced, Germany and her Allies shall submit their military, naval, and air policies to the supervision of the Allied High Commission provided for in Article V of this treaty. In addition to the powers specified above, this Commission shall have power to limit the production of armaments and munitions of war in those states and to regulate the importation of war material into them.

Sec. 5. The provisions of this Article shall be binding upon Germany and her Allies until they are admitted into the League of States.

Article III

REPARATION

Section 1. On the basis of reparation for damage done during the war through loss of life, limb, or property to the civilian populations of the Allies, on land, by sea, or from the air, Germany shall make compensation to the Allied Powers in the following amounts:

Belgium, $3,800,000,000; France, $7,000,000,000; Serbia, $2,400,000,000; Rumania, $1,000,000,000; Great Britain, $3,400,000,000; Italy, $2,000,000,000.

Sec. 2. This reparation shall be paid at the rate of one-half billion dollars per year, payments being due March 28 of each year, beginning with 1920; provided that Germany shall be allowed ten years in which to pay the first five billion dollars; provided further that on any one of the first ten yearly payments which is not paid when due interest shall accrue at the rate of six per cent. per annum until payment of principal and interest is made.

Sec. 3. The aforesaid payments of reparation shall be apportioned to the Allied Nations named in Section 1 of this Article in the proportion which the amount of each nation's reparation bears to the total amount of reparation.

Article IV

TERRITORIAL ADJUSTMENTS

Section 1. Germany shall return the Malmedy District to Belgium.

Sec. 2. Germany shall return Alsace-Lorraine to France.

Sec. 3. The region between the Rhine River and Alsace-Lorraine shall be completely defortified and shall be free from military operations by both France and Germany. The creation of a Rhenish Republic as a buffer state would be contrary to the principle of self-determination of states.

Sec. 4. The Trentino shall be restored to Italy.

Sec. 5. Jugo-Slavia is hereby recognized as comprising Serbia, Montenegro, Herzegovina, Dalmatia, Bosnia, Croatia, Slavonia, Carniola, Istria, and the Banat.

Sec. 6. Czecho-Slovakia is hereby recognized as comprising Bohemia, Moravia, Silesia, and those sections of Upper Hungary and Tatra district that were the crown-lands of Austria.

Sec. 7. That portion of Macedonia known as Tchamara and northern Epirus shall be added to Albania.

Sec. 8. Bessarabia, Bukowina, Transylvania, and that part of the Banat of Temesvár which is inhabited by Rumanians shall be added to Rumania.

Sec. 9. Those parts of Epirus, Thrace, and Macedonia which have not been added to Albania by the terms of this treaty shall be added to Greece.

Sec. 10. Turkish, Russian, and Persian Armenia are hereby recognized as the nation of Armenia and shall be subject to the mandatory provisions of Article VI of this treaty.

Sec. 11. That portion of the former Austrian Empire which is predominantly German shall be added to Germany.

Sec. 12. Kiaochow shall be returned to China.

Sec. 13. Poland shall be recognized as comprising East Prussia, West Prussia, Posen and those portions of the Old Polish State which were taken by Austria and Prussia.

Sec. 14. Under the provisions of Article XI, Section 6, of this treaty, a High Commission shall be appointed which, acting as the agent of the League of States, shall give such advice and assistance to Poland, Czecho-Slovakia, and Jugo-Slavia as in the judgment of the commission the circumstances warrant.

Article V

HIGH COMMISSION TO DEAL WITH
GERMANY AND HER ALLIES

Section 1. Under the provisions of Article XI, Section 6, of this treaty a High Commission shall be appointed with authority to act for the Allied Powers in the execution of this treaty insofar as it relates to Germany and her Allies.

Sec. 2. This High Commission shall have power to appoint the commission provided for in Article I of this treaty and such other commissions as it may deem advisable in order to carry out the provisions of this treaty with respect to Germany and her Allies.

Article VI

MANDATORIES

Under the provisions of Article XI, Section 6 of this treaty, the following mandatories are established:

Section 1. Great Britain for Arabia, Persia, German East Africa and German Southwest Africa.

Sec. 2. France for Syria, the Ukraine, Togo, and Kamerun.

Sec. 3. The United States of America for Armenia, Albania, and Mesopotamia.

Sec. 4. Japan for the Caroline and the Marshall Islands.

Sec. 5. Australia for New Guinea.

Sec. 6. New Zealand for Samoa.

Sec. 7. Sweden for Finland.

Sec. 8. Norway for Lithuania.

Article VII

ECONOMIC POLICY

Section 1. Each individual nation shall determine according to its usual methods its economic policy towards Germany and her Allies. Economic policy is here defined as policy with respect to free trade, open markets, commercial boycotts, and tariffs.

Sec. 2. France shall be given predominant use of the coal and iron mines in the Saar valley until her own supply of coal and iron is again available, details of this predominance to be determined by the Allied High Commission.

Article VIII

POLICY TOWARDS RUSSIA

Section 1. Under the provisions of Article XI, Section 6, of this treaty, a High Commission shall be appointed to study internal conditions in Russia, to handle international economic transactions with Russia, and to act as agent through which the Russian people may receive supplies of food, machinery, and other necessaries from the nations of the world.

Sec. 2. This Commission shall extend to any government in Russia, any economic support it may deem necessary, provided such government will assume responsibility for its international obligations, and can furnish credit. The ability of such government to make good its international obligations and the soundness of its credit shall be determined by the Commission.

Sec. 3. The Commission shall endeavor to co-ordinate the people of Russia into one government by consulting and advising with the various factions, and by the use of such propaganda as it sees fit. After having studied the situation in Russia, if the Commission finds or succeeds in establishing a government that has elements of stability and character which it believes will triumph over all factions in Russia, it shall concentrate its economic and political support on this government, until Russia shall enter the League of States.

Article IX

KIEL CANAL AND DARDANELLES

Section 1. The Kiel Canal and the Dardanelles shall be defortified to the extent deemed necessary by the Commission appointed under the provisions of Article II of this treaty.

Sec. 2. The Kiel Canal and the Dardanelles shall be internationalized under the provisions of Article XI, Section 10, of this treaty.

Article X

RECOGNITION OF AUTHORITY OF LEAGUE OF NATIONS

Section 1. In order to create an agency by which the provisions of the preceding articles may be executed through concerted action, and in order to promote the interests of civilization by decreasing the causes of war and by providing machinery for preventing war, the Allied Powers hereby agree to the following Constitution of the League of States, and Germany and her Allies hereby recognize the government that shall be established under the provisions of the Constitution of the League of States as the duly authorized agent of the Allied Powers in enforcing the terms of this treaty, except as otherwise provided by the treaty.

Article XI

Constitution of the League of States

SECTION 1

MEMBERSHIP

Paragraph 1. After the organization of this League of States any free state of the world that has a responsible and stable government and is able and willing to give effective guarantees of loyal intention to observe its covenants may be admitted by a two-thirds vote of the General Conference.

Par. 2. For the purposes of membership in the League of States, the peoples of the world are divided into three classes, as follows:

(1) Those peoples that are capable of assuming immediately the responsibilities and duties of membership in the League.

(2) Those peoples that are temporarily incapable of membership in the League, but that are capable of a large degree of self-government, and that with such assistance as the League may be able to afford through commissions, give promise of being fit, at an early date, for membership in the League. Such peoples shall be admitted to the League as soon as they can comply with the provisions of Paragraph 1 of this section.

(3) Those peoples whose lack of development requires that, for the protection of their own best interests, they be temporarily assigned as mandates to some member state of the League. Such peoples shall be admitted to the second class as soon as they manifest that degree of development that will make it possible for the League to deal directly with them by means of commissions, and shall be admitted as members of the League as soon as they can comply with Paragraph 1 of this section.

SECTION 2

BRANCHES OF GOVERNMENT

Paragraph 1. The government of the League shall be vested in a General Conference and an Executive Council.

Par. 2. The General Conference shall be composed of representatives from such of the following states as shall ratify this constitution, to be apportioned as follows: The United States of America, Great Britain, France, Italy, and Japan, five each; Belgium and Brazil, three each; China, Greece, Rumania, Norway, and Sweden, two each; Cuba, Guatemala, Hayti, Honduras, Liberia, Siam, and Portugal, one each. Each of these states shall determine the method of election, qualifications, and length of term of its representatives.

Par. 3. The Executive Council shall be composed of one representative from each of the following states: The United States of America, the British Empire, France, Italy, and Japan; and four representatives from the other states represented in the General Conference. The method of selection, qualifications, and length of term of the representatives from the United States, the British Empire,

France, Italy, and Japan shall be determined by those states individually. At the first meeting of the General Conference the representatives of the other member states shall elect the four representatives to which they are entitled collectively on the Executive Council. These representatives shall be elected for terms of one, two, three, and four years, respectively. Thereafter one representative shall be elected in each year in the manner just provided for a four-year term.

Par. 4. Whenever other states shall be admitted to the League, the General Conference shall determine whether they shall be represented individually by one representative on the Executive Council, or whether they shall join in the election of the four representatives as provided in Paragraph 3 of this section. The General Conference shall also fix the representation of such newly admitted states in the General Conference, provided that such representation shall not exceed five for any one state. These representatives shall be elected as provided in Paragraph 2 of this section.

SECTION 3
OFFICERS

Paragraph 1. The officers of the General Conference shall be a President, a Vice-President, and a Secretary. The officers of the Executive Council shall be a Chairman and a Secretary.

Par. 2. The President and the Vice-President of the General Conference shall be elected by that body and shall hold office for a term of three years subject to an unlimited number of re-elections. The Secretary shall be elected to hold office according to the will of the Conference.

Par. 3. The Chairman of the Executive Council shall be elected by its members from among themselves to hold office for one year subject to an unlimited number of re-elections. The Secretary shall be elected to hold office according to the will of the Council.

SECTION 4
MEETINGS

Paragraph 1. The first meeting of the General Conference and of the Executive Council shall be held at Versailles. At this meeting the General Conference shall select a permanent seat of the government, at which later meetings of these two bodies shall be held, except when either of these bodies at its own discretion shall choose to meet elsewhere.

Par. 2. The General Conference shall convene once a year, and shall remain in session as long as it deems necessary. The President shall have power to call extraordinary sessions of the Conference whenever necessary.

Par. 3. The Executive Council shall meet at stated intervals to be determined by itself, and at other times when necessary, upon the call of the Chairman, and shall remain in session as long as it deems necessary.

SECTION 5
THE GENERAL CONFERENCE

Paragraph 1. The General Conference shall have power to make necessary laws securing to the members of this League freedom of transportation by land for legitimate commercial purposes of an international scope, but the Conference may provide for the levying and enforcement through the Executive Council of commercial and social blockades.

Par. 2. The General Conference shall have power to regulate and provide for the payment of the salaries of the members of the General Conference and of the Executive Council and for the payment of the salaries and expenses, if considered necessary, of such other persons as shall be necessary to carry out the provisions of this Constitution; and to apportion these, together with other necessary expenses of the League, among the member states in proportion to their representation in the General Conference.

Par. 3. The General Conference shall have power to limit, at its first meeting, the military and naval forces of the member states to the strength required for the adequate protection of the several states individually and of the League of States as a whole, and to alter these limits from time to time thereafter, as it shall deem advisable.

Par. 4. The General Conference shall have power to limit the military and naval forces of new member states as they shall be admitted to the League and to alter these limits from time to time as it shall deem advisable.

Par. 5. The General Conference shall have power to secure the freedom of international communication by means of telegraph, telephone, cable, and postal facilities.

SECTION 6
THE EXECUTIVE COUNCIL

Paragraph 1. It shall be the duty of the Executive Council to enforce this Constitution and international law as formulated by the General Conference, and the entire land and naval forces of the member states shall be at its disposal for this purpose.

Par. 2. It shall be the duty of the Executive Council to appoint all commissions herein provided for.

SECTION 7

Paragraph 1. In the future, whenever the General Conference shall deem it necessary, it shall appoint a mandatory power for any territory or people, but only after consulting the latter in regard to the appointment.

Par. 2. For such mandates as were appointed under Article IV of this treaty, or as shall be appointed under Paragraph 1 of this section, the following principle shall be adhered to:

The General Conference shall delegate to the selected mandatory power a certain degree of authority and control which shall be set forth by the General Conference under a special act or charter. This act or charter shall reserve to the

General Conference complete power of ultimate control and supervision, as well as the right of appeal to the General Conference by the territory or people against any gross breach of the mandate by the mandatory state. Any state or territory that has been placed under a mandate shall reserve the right to itself to regulate its commerce and trade with other nations.

SECTION 8
INTERNATIONAL DISPUTES

Paragraph 1. Whenever a dispute arises between member states which they cannot settle by ordinary diplomatic methods, the Executive Council shall immediately take cognizance of the dispute and shall attempt to effect a settlement by means of mediation or conciliation.

Par. 2. If a settlement of the dispute cannot be effected by means of mediation or conciliation, the Executive Council shall appoint a board of arbitration which shall make thorough investigation of the dispute and render its decision within six months.

Par. 3. This decision shall be binding on all parties to the controversy.

Par. 4. The states involved shall refrain from hostilities before the dispute is submitted to the Executive Council or to the board of arbitration, while the dispute is under consideration, and after a decision has been reached.

SECTION 9

Paragraph 1. All peaceful vessels are free to traverse the seas of the world.

Par. 2. Private property belonging to individuals shall not be seized or destroyed except when belligerent nations use individuals as instruments in transporting contraband.

Par. 3. Ships carrying contraband shall be subject to seizure, provided they are carried before a properly constituted prize-court, said court to be appointed by the Executive Council. The duty of said prize-court shall be to determine whether the vessel carried contraband, and if so, to award such vessel to its captor.

Par. 4. No neutral port or coast shall be blockaded.

Par. 5. The use of submarines outside territorial waters against passenger or merchant ships is forbidden.

Par. 6. "Territorial waters" include all national waterways as defined in paragraph 3 in Section 10 and all other waters to a distance of twenty-five miles from the coast of any state except as limited by paragraph 1 of section 10.

SECTION 10

Paragraph 1. All bodies of water less than fifty miles in width that do not have their source and outlet within the boundaries of any one state, that are controlled jointly or totally by the members of the League of States, and that are navigated by vessels of more than 1,000 tons displacement are declared to be international waterways.

Par. 2. The League of States guarantees all member nations equal rights and privileges on all international waterways.

Par. 3. The Kiel Canal and Dardanelles shall be international waterways.

Par. 4. International waterways shall be fortified to that minimum that in the opinion of the League of States is consistent with national and international safety.

Par. 5. The League of States guarantees the neutrality of international waterways, prohibits warfare being carried on in international waterways and guarantees that all nations bordering on such waterways shall be free from aggression or invasion from the side of said waterways.

SECTION 11

NON-MEMBER STATES

Paragraph 1. Whenever any dispute shall arise between a member of this League and any non-member state that cannot be settled by ordinary diplomatic methods the Executive Council shall attempt to effect a settlement of the dispute by means of mediation or conciliation. Failing to effect a settlement by such means, the Executive Council shall direct that the dispute be submitted to a board of arbitration as provided in Article VII, and when a decision is rendered it

Local Solons Consider Plans for Universal Peace and Other Things

The Peace Conference in English 21 is making excellent progress in the work of drawing up a constitution for the League of Nations. Mr. Gwynn, Chairman of the Constitutional Committee, has submitted the first draft for the consideration of the Conference. The fourteen articles embodied therein were discussed thoroughly by the Conference. Debate was spirited and intelligent, showing that the men representing the different nations have acquired a large and accurate stock of knowledge about international politics, conditions, and policies, and the conflicting claims and aspirations of the various nations. Sharp contention over many points made it very evident that several compromises, amendments and additions will be necessary before the final adoption of the constitution. The committee is drafting the new form; and it is hoped that it can be adopted by Monday. It was planned to have this constitution completed before the constitution drawn up by the Peace Conference in Paris was made public. It is very noticeable that in this matter, and indeed in all of its work, this Conference has avoided servile imitation of the Conference in Paris. Using all available information on the international situation and problems it has tried to make its own settlement of these problems.

Following the adoption of the constitution the Conference will take up in order the question of indemnities, territorial claims, colonial adjustments freedom of the seas and international trade relations. The principle upon which indemnities are to be imposed has already been discussed by the Conference, and each nation has presented its claims. When the question comes up again for its final settlefent, Mr. Wolfe, head of the Committee on Indemnities, will propose a concrete settlement of each claim for the consideration of the Conference. In order to get the different topics of each subject before the Conference at the proper time and lose no time in useless talk, the Program Committee, headed by Mr. York, presents each week a schedule of the work for the

(Continued on Page 4)

LOCAL SOLONS CONSIDER PLANS FOR UNIVERSAL PEACE AND OTHER THINGS
(Continued from Page 1)

week, which is adopted by the Conference. Part of the available time is used for set speeches from the different delegations; the rest is used for general discussion or debate. Dr. Greenlaw is pleased with the work of this group, which he regards as excellent training for thoroughness in research and exposition and speed and intelligence in debating.

Tar Heel, February 14, 1919; see the second paragraph. North Carolina Collection, University of North Carolina at Chapel Hill

shall be binding on both parties to the controversy. In case the non-member state shall commence hostilities against the member state before a decision shall have been rendered by the board of arbitration, or in case it shall refuse to abide by the decision of the court, the Executive Council shall enforce compliance with the decision as provided in Section 6.

Par. 2. Whenever a dispute shall arise between non-member states, the Executive Council shall offer its services to bring about an amicable settlement, but it shall take no steps to compel the disputing states to submit their dispute to the Executive Council for settlement, nor to enforce any decision that may be rendered if the controversy is submitted to mediation, conciliation, or arbitration. The Executive Council shall, however, use such means at its disposal as shall be necessary to protect the interests of the members of the League from injury by belligerent non-member states.

SECTION 12
TREATIES

Paragraph 1. There shall be no secret treaties between any of the members of this League.

Par. 2. No member of this League shall make a secret treaty with any non-member state.

SECTION 13
WITHDRAWAL

Par. 1. No member state shall be allowed to withdraw from the League.

SECTION 14
RATIFICATION OF CONSTITUTION

Paragraph 1. The ratification of this Constitution by any four of the following states: The United States of America, the British Empire, France, Italy, and Japan, with or without any of the other states mentioned in Section 2 of this Constitution, shall be sufficient for the establishment of this League of States as provided herein.

Par. 2. Following the ratification of this Constitution by any four of the states named in Paragraph 1, the states so ratifying shall each appoint one delegate to meet at Versailles within two months, and those delegates shall make the necessary preliminary arrangements for the establishment of the League.

SECTION 15
AMENDMENTS

Paragraph 1. The General Conference, whenever two-thirds of the members thereof shall deem it necessary, shall propose amendments to this Constitution, which, when ratified by the legislative bodies of three-fourths of the member states, provided that any amendment to be adopted must be ratified by at least four of the following nations: The United States of America, Great Britain, France, Italy, and Japan, shall be considered to all intents and purposes as part of this Constitution.

Appendix B

Debate Speeches

Debate was an important activity at the university. Thomas Wolfe was elected vice-president of the Freshman Debating Club ("Freshman Debating Club Perfects Organization," *Tar Heel*, October 7, 1916, 1, 5) and was an active campus speaker during his college years.

M.J.B.

Speech Advocating Preparation for War, 1916

The eleven-page typescript revised in Wolfe's hand is in the William B. Wisdom Collection, Houghton Library, Harvard University. Obvious typing errors have been corrected by the editors, but words have not been emended or supplied.
Written in 1916 by Tom Wolfe [Wolfe's hand]

MR. PRESIDENT, ladies and gentlemen and Honorable Judges, we have arrived at a crisis in our national affairs. Democracy stands at the crossroads. In this broad America of God and Man, here, where not a few men, not a family, but mankind, shall say where we shall be; here, I ask, shall it be peace or shall it be war?

Today there is a great question before us. Shall we deliberately say to ourselves that we believe force has now become the dominating factor of the world and that moral issues and our own national ideals of liberty and freedom have passed into disuse; that we have returned to that state of civilization in which we may consider no nation a friend, but every nation a potential enemy, that we must therefore be armed to the extent of our ability; that we who were warned by the great father of his country against entangling alliances are now to become a part of the most terrible alliance known to humanity – an alliance with militarism, under a system by which English capital makes torpedoes for Turks to destroy Englishmen, and German capital makes guns and shells for Servians to take German lives.

In short, gentlemen, we are asked to be prepared for war. For what war I ask and with whom? With Great Britain? As long as a hundred million Americans have arms, and an undefended border line between us and ten million Canadians we need not fear the biggest navy in the world which stands back of them. Then, too, Great Britain has signed a treaty to wait a year before going to war with us and to submit any dispute to neutral investigation. France and Russia have made the same promise. They too will keep their word. A treaty has never been violated by either of these nations and has never been considered in any sense to be a mere scrap of paper.

Shall we prepare to defend the great, rich country against little Japan, whose citizens are even now groaning under an enormous debt? We have twice her population and ten times her wealth. We have the best credit in the world and 6,000 miles of salt water separates Japan's navy from a navy which is declared by the best experts to be twice as efficient. Shall we prepare to fight Germany? We have 35% more people than Germany, 200% more wealth and 3,000 miles to ocean lie between us. How could Germany spare even a single regiment to send 3,000 miles beyond the sea to attack us, even if she wanted to? She well knows that when she makes any hostile invasion she leaves her own country a prey to an iron ring of 450,000,000 foes regularly awaiting a chance to override her.

Those who assume as a matter of course, that Germany (or any other nation) could invade this country with great ease are victims of the wildest and most fanciful delusion.

While it was taking a fleet of 100 fast ships six months to transport 1000,000 soldiers to our shores we could be doing something in the way of defense. We are the only great nation that can live upon itself and by itself. We can't be starved, we can't be deprived of clothing, we can't be robbed of our fuel and iron. America I say is the only nation where true preparedness exists. In it are great munition factories capable of equipping entire armies in a few days. Its complete and compact railroad system is transporting gigantic forces from one boundary of the country to the other. Its natural fortifications governed by Neptune, are unsurpassed. Judges, it seems to me that America is invincible, and yet in view of all this a great movement toward an utterly undemocratic imperialism is daily gaining in strength, leaving behind it a large number of highly honorable and thoroly disinterested men none the less misguided because of their own good intentions. Unfortunately, such men are utilized by forces that are anything but patriotic and disinterested – the forces of war traffickers and munition makers the world over. These men are asking that we be prepared at a time when we would seem safer than at any other period of our history, at a time when Europe is bleeding to death; at a time when all our time, money and efforts should be expended in binding up their broken wounds instead of considering how to embark on a course that would bring us the love and gratitude of every nation, such, for instance as taxing ourselves a billion dollars to retrieve their lost civilization. When this bloody struggle is over, we prepare a policy which will inevitably make each of them hate us a little more, a policy based on the false philosophy that might makes right.

Before entering into any new policy of preparedness it would seem only the part of wisdom to begin with a study of what we have and an official statement of its military value. So it is that Congressman Kitchin, majority leader in the House bases his opposition to the President's bill squarely on that fact that our navy is superior to German's and twice as effective as Japan's and stakes his honor on the accuracy of these facts. He uses as his authority three of the most prominent Admiral's in the navy, Badger, Winterhafter and Fletcher, all of whom testified before a house committee that our navy was superior to Germany. In proof of this, the last five dreadnoughts authorized by Congress are superior to any six dreadnoughts Germany has built or building. Our ships are stronger, larger and more heavily armored; our guns are larger, stronger and more effective. Of the big guns of the ships twelve inches and over we have 284 and Germany has only 194.

Gentlemen, the real struggle of this great war is not between military Germany and the Allies. The supreme and vital issues of this century are between Law and Anarchy. Anarchy is the rule of men by force and by fear. Militarism is anarchy. Anarchy is chaos and ruin.

War between civilized and Christian nations is as senseless as it is foul and wicked. There is no dispute so small that nations will not fight for it, if they want to fight. There is no dispute so far reaching that it cannot be settled with peace and with <u>honor</u> if the nations wish to be just and fair. If, according to the testimony of our best experts we have a navy superior to any in the world except Great Britain, against whom do we propose to prepare. The naval appropriations during the present administration, so far, exceeds by $500,000 the entire approximations of Tedy Roosevelt's last term, and equals the amount spent during Taft's four years. Our coast defenses are the finest in existence; on the authority of two of the greatest living experts, General Erasmas A. Weaver, and Gen. Wm. Crozier – General Weaver said "My information is that our system of fortification are reasonably adequate for all defensive purposes which they are likely to meet" and further said "I have been a close student of the whole subject for a number of years and I know of no fortifications in the world so far as my reading, observation and knowledge goes that compare favorably in efficiency with ours. General Crozier in considering alterations now being made to our guns said "In my opinion these guns with the other advantages which our land defense fortifications have will be adequate for maintaining a successful combat with vessels of war armed with any gun which is now under construction. I am of the opinion, Mr. Chairman, that they will be of such power naval officers will not put their ships against them in a fight." It is known also on reliable and expert testimony that no navy can operate at more than 50% of its strength at 4,000 miles from its base. Furthermore, I quote Napoleon Bonaparte who said no over seas invasion could be successful until every ship of the enemy was sunk.

So it is, Judges, that instead of possessing the insignificant defenses our opponents could have you believe we develop into huge and powerful proportions when our true status is observed.

I believe submarines and mines will answer largely the question of our defensive preparedness. If a few submarines can protect the German navy against a fleet four times as large and as powerful why couldn't submarines protect our fleet and our coasts with equal assurance? I may add, for the benefit of any opponents, that we possess more submarines than Germany. Surely in view of all this there can be no possible excuse for haste in legislation.

If my audience will bear with me a few minutes I will deal in some dry statistics to show how astoundingly far-reaching is the President's program.

We are spending annually, getting ready for war, over $250,000,000 that is, over ten times what we spend, annually, on agriculture. But the jingoes and militarists are not satisfied. They say we have been negligent of our country's safety; that we must now begin to get ready in earnest. To hear some of our new born fire eaters it would be thought that we have been absolutely deaf to all militant appeals, yet between 1881 and 1915 our enormous naval budget has increased from $13,000,000 to $150,000,000, i.e., we are spending annually seven times the endowment of Yale or Harvard Universities with nothing to show for it after 15 years when the dreadnoughts of today will be relegated to the scrap heap, or be shot to pieces as junk.

Now in view of the fact that we have a navy superior to any in the world, except Great Britain's, in view of the fact the navy is growing larger, stronger, better equipped, and more efficient than ever before, in view of the fact, as the President declared a little more than a year ago to Congress; "We are threatened from no source," this program increases at one bound in one year, increases our already immensely large naval appropriations more than our total increase for the last fourteen years, more than the increase by Germany the whole 15 years preceding this war, and more than the combined increase of all the nations in the world in any one year of their history (in times of peace). The five year program increases our naval appropriation over forty times more than the increase by Germany in five years preceding the European War, and $200,000,000 more than the increase of all the nations in the world for five years preceding this war, and $50,000,000 more than all the nations in the world for the ten years preceding the war.

Furthermore, we were spending on our navy prior to this war from $20,000,000 to $30,000,000 more annually than any nation in the world, except Great Britain. Forty thousand millions of dollars is a sum so vast that the mention of it leaves only a blurred impression on the mind, yet that is about what the nations have paid in a single century for the folly and wickedness of their quarrels and fightings. And this is not the whole of the huge "Butcher's Bill." Speaking, for the last time from a monetary standpoint, the condition of the treasury will not warrant any new naval appropriations budget. Our general surplus fund of $150,000,000 has reached the vanishing point. We have been forced to levy an emergency tax, our defects still exist, our revenues are still insufficient. Let us, then make haste slowly to tax this over-burdened people more. If there ever was a time in our history when Congress, the administration and the people, should consider any new policy with calmness and deliberation, – it is now.

Among all the programs for preparedness, now agitating the public mind, none seems to have noticed our neglect of the nations most-essential defense. In the midst of all this mad frenzy to get ready for a foreign foe, we are blind to the fact that we are not getting our citizens ready even for peace. We content ourselves with a 5th rate civilization. It takes five years and $15,000,000 to make a warship ready to be sunk by the next submarine. It takes 21 years and perhaps $5,000 to make a citizen ready to cope with any problem in peace or war. Yet we plunge into the battleship proposition with zeal and vigor, but leave the citizenship investment to solve itself. Our army of illiterate youth is about twice the size of the standing army we are urged to train and equip for national defense. And every one of those 820,000 children against whom the schoolhouse door is closed, who bend daily over the whirling spindles and at night "homeward plot their way," form the potential tool of this nation's enemy's to blow this Democracy's boasted institutions into scrap form.

GENTLEMEN, if true preparedness is desired, the true preparedness of strong, robust, stalwart manhood, let it be obtained by spending the price of a few dreadnoughts upon those 600,000 Americans who die annually from preventable accidents and disease. If those gentlemen who declare in our halls of Congress that we too should enter the ignoble strife, will devote their labor, and their eloquence to the kind of preparedness I have suggested, then I too will be a devoted follower of their program. But I will not heed the pleas of the munition makers, and those of the insidious war <u>Lobby</u>.

The military men of this nation have no more right to regulate the size of the army and navy than have the protected manufacturers of this country the right to regulate the tariffs, and to say, thereby, how much money shall blow into their own pockets.

I am opposed to the so-called preparedness program because it is unnecessary, because it endangers our most precious institutions, and because in the final analysis no one can measure its cost. This policy of military preparedness which some desire to force upon us is not new. It has been tried consistently for 6,000 years.

It smashed eventually Egypt, Greece, Rome, Spain, and France, as world empires. It is now bearing its logical fruit in Europe, ruining commerce, agriculture, manufacture, and all human enterprise in a tornado of folly. When gentlemen therefore urge Uncle Sam to adopt the <u>precise</u> policy that is devastating Europe, he shows the soundest sort of common sense when he declares emphatically NO.

For America is the humanitarian of nations. Her ideals are the ideals of liberty, civilization, and christianity. Upon her decision in large measure depends the world's decision to advance or to retreat in civilization. The whole world turns to her for advice. And yet she is planning to descend from her present high position to wallow in the mire with the rest.

The honor America now enjoys as a world power, has not come by her sending a white squadron of warships around the world, but because she paid helpless Spain $20,000,000 for the Phillipines, because she returned the Boxer indemnity to China, because she refused to interpret the Panama Canal to our own advantage and because we have spent ourselves and our money the world over in relieving suffering. Let us, not then succumb to the theory that might makes right. Armaments are a challenge. If we arm, another nation arms, and so the mad race goes on with neither gaining permanent advantage but both paying the bill. Let no true American believe that there is anything in the terrors abroad to make us abjure the wisest teachings of our fathers, or fore-fathers, and the founders of this great republic.

A perpetual peace is no longer a dream, but it looms on War's dark horizon as a splendid reality. This should be an age of peace, not of war, of defense not of destruction, of life, not of death. War has had its place in history. The despot <u>Must</u> Go "Who wades through slaughter to a throne and shuts the gates of mercy on mankind." Let us arm for peace for the day,

> "When the war drums beat no longer,
> When the battle flags are furl'd,
> In the parliament of man,
> The Federation of the World."
>
> Tom Wolfe [signed]

Speech against Federal Ownership of Railways, 1917

The seven-page typescript revised in Wolfe's hand is in the William B. Wisdom Collection, Houghton Library, Harvard University.

MR. PRESIDENT AND GENTLEMEN OF THE SOCIETY:

No more important problem confronts the people of this nation, than the question of what policy they shall pursue in future with the railroads of this country. It is the most intricate, delicate and far reaching of all our great national issues. When you think of the extent of the American railways in mileage, equipment, service; when you consider the money invested in them, you will perceive that here is a question that must be handled with the utmost care and deliberation of this entire American nation; a question which deals with a great branch of our national life. It is my purpose to show you that the method some propose, govt. ownership, would be not only costly, unnecessary, and [   ], but that it would be dangerous to the highest degree.

In arguing this question, it must not be assumed that the private railway corporations have no connection with the government. The railroads of this country are regulated by a strict and comprehensive government system known as the Interstate Commerce Commission. Any citizen with a grievance can appeal to this commission and get a speedy, just and sympathetic hearing. Therefore, gentlemen, the change that some advocate, would not be a change from strictly private ownership to public ownership, but rather a chance from government supervision to government ownership.

The supporters of government ownership maintain that it would reduce operating expenses and that the cost of rendering service would be lowered. In fact, this is one of their chief arguments. Let us first consider this contention and decide whether or not this government is capable of reducing the cost of service.

For years the people of this nation have been struggling under a most vicious system of political distribution. There is one bill in particular that is a masterpiece of Congressional "log-rolling." This is known as the rivers and harbors bill. We can never have a sane, safe and rational system of public works – under present methods. For it seems as if our legislators have lost all broad national vision, and have narrowed their perspective down to local affairs.

When the government wastes money on fruitless waterway projects, it is forced to pay interest on the investment.

If it should make enormous and extravagant expenditures on the railways, it would both have to pay interest on the investment and the expense of operating them. Political distribution causes money to be spent where it is not needed, and diverts it where it is needed. Under government ownership, passenger stations would be public buildings, and if our legislators followed custom, large amounts would be wasted on costly and useless stations. If appropriations for railroads were distributed thro the various congressional districts as are other appropriations, fixed charges would be greatly increased. No one can estimate how much more expenses would be under public than under private management. At any rate the difference would devour any profits that might be made, unless Congressional methods underwent a revolution.

In short, gentlemen, under government ownership you put the railroads in charge of a group of men, who, in many cases, work only for selfish, local interests; men who have not the same incentive to reduce expenses as the head of a private corporation would have. Officers of a government railway system would be men of less force and ability than are the higher salaried corporation heads. They would have one great evil to combat that private heads do not have, i.e. political influence. Thirty-five years ago a government commission in Italy, after the most thorough investigation ever made, decided that government ownership was more costly than private ownership. It cannot be said that conditions have changed. On the contrary, the evidence I have brought out, would seem to point out that public ownership in this country would be much less economical than private ownership. These reasons alone, gentlemen, ought to be sufficient argument against government ownership. But we will not stop here. Another leading contention of those supporting public ownership is relative to the quality of service. I point out that the quality of service on American railroads has been made possible by the keen competition existing between the different systems. Under government ownership, competition would be entirely abolished. It could not exist between two lines operated by the same corporation. Travelers and shippers could not stimulate competition by giving their patronage to the line that rendered best service.

Comparing the railroads service in the United States, we find it is equally as good and probably better than any government owned railway in the world. Both in freight car capacity provided per mile of line, and in the ratio of the freight car capacity, the United States leads all other nations.

The nature of service under government ownership depends on the zeal of the officers for promoting it; officers who would not have the same object in pleasing the people as have the competing private lines. Under fairly comparable conditions, the private railways furnish easily as adequate and as good service as any state railway.

It has been argued that since government ownership is successful in some countries it would be successful here. The two nations most often quoted, are Germany and Japan. These countries, however, must not be considered. Germany is governed by a military system, and nearly all the railway employees are reserves and could be sent to the colors at any time. Japan, also a military nation, follows the same system. A labor union is an unknown element to the employee in these countries. The United States is a non-military nation. No military influence may be exercised over the employes of a government railway system in this country. Take into consideration, gentlemen, that there exists in those countries that use government ownership with success, a form and code of government quite different from ours. We must bear in mind that what is a good system for a nation with one set of conditions may not be beneficial for a nation with a set of conditions entirely different. For this reason no comparison can be made.

However, we may take the case of France, a nation which has a government in many respects similar to ours. The Western Railway, of France, was the last road purchased by that Government. The transfer from private to public management was made in 1908. By 1913 operating expenses had increased 52%. In the meantime freight and passenger rates have remained the same. The situation in France is instructive because we may study this question under practically the same conditions that exist in our own country.

The condition of labor is a favorite bone of contention for those supportering government ownership. And yet the most reliable statistics show us that railroad employes are the highest paid class of men in this country. The figures show further that with living expenses from 25% to 65% higher in this country than abroad, the railway employes receive from 80% to 160% higher wages than do the employes of any foreign railway, whether owned by the public or by a private corporation. But let us admit that under government ownership, wages would be increased. Is this an argument for adopting it? No, it is rather one against it.

The higher wages paid and perhaps were more, the increase in the number of men employed would increase operating expenses. The public would be forced to bear the brunt of the increased expenses. In short, one particular class of men would be benefited at the expense of the entire nation. The fact that railroad employes might get higher wages is not an argument for the welfare of the public, for the working class as a whole, for the adoption of government ownership.

There is one more contention made by the advocates of government ownership, and this concerns the making of the rates. But will the rates be lower under public than under private ownership? Let us consider the great danger. Govern-

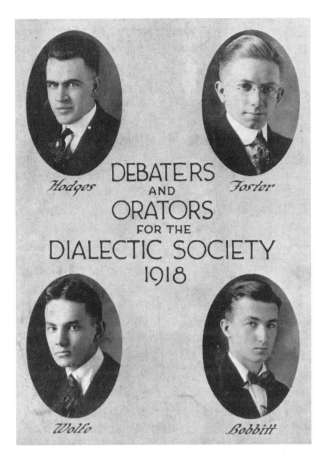

North Carolina Collection, University of North Carolina
at Chapel Hill

ment ownership would put the making of the rates of an enormous government
into a bureau of officials unfamilar with local and general conditions, and without individual interest in the management of railroads.

Under private ownership, railroad managers have for years been making an
honest effort to perfect their system, so as to render the best and cheapest possible
service. If the government is to run the railroads, intelligent people will demand
that they be run at a lower rate than before. And the consensus of intelligent
opinion is that rates are lower here than abroad.

Gentlemen, we owe a great and lasting debt to the railroads of this country,
– Roads that have been constructed and operated by private capital. Under private ownership the development of railways in this country has gone forward at
a rate that has never been equalled in any nation. Without these railroads, three
fourths of the vast territory of this country would still be barren. [Here]

The prosperity of the American system and the excellency of its service is undeniable. If a lasting change is to be made, it must certainly be made for good reasons. Are there sufficient reasons to induce us to violate the great American democratic principle that government ownership ought not to own and operate what private ownership can run and operate? Such a change is so revolutionary and so undemocratic that evidence must show that private ownership has been an absolute failure. And I challenge anyone to prove this. [Here]

I am opposed to government ownership of railroads because it is unnecessary, because it is unfair, and because, in the last and in the true analysis no one can measure its cost.

I have endeavored to present this question in a fair, just and unbiased manner. And I have arrived at the foregoing conclusions.

Gentlemen, the issue stands squarely before you. There can be no possible evasion of the facts. Now, after having the true evidence, are you, as stockholders in a great corporation, willing to burden yourselves with an additional national debt of at least $20,000,000,000.? Are you willing to incorporate in a single department of your government, an army of over a million and a half of men – more than is contained in every other branch of government?

This is what government ownership means. It means these things and many others much more serious.

In a few years, you gentlemen will be forced to make your stand in one direction or the other. And with the consciousness of true and just citizenship upon you, with the knowledge of what government ownership really means I know beforehand what your answer will be.

My friends, let nothing deceive you. Consider the great nation in which you now live, its resources, its wealth and prosperity. Private railroads have made it all that it is. And when the time comes when you, as a citizen, must make your stand, in full confidence of the unalterable truth, fight with all this strength that is in you, against that awful folly which urges you to abolish a system that has contributed most to your progress, prosperity and happiness.

FINIS

Speech on Internationalism, 1919

This speech is probably related to Wolfe's participation in the English 21 Peace Treaty project ("Solons Gather around the Festive Board in a Joyous Love-Feast," Tar Heel, March 28, 1919, 1, 3).

The five-page manuscript is in the William B. Wisdom Collection, Houghton Library, Harvard University.

Mr Chairman;

Yesterday, after that eventful session, I was approached by one of the members of the Russian delegation, Count I Dontnowhosky, and reproached for refusing to allow myself to be dominated by pure principle – for proposing, in fine, a compromise between Principle and Expediency. But, Mr President, while we are talking most magnificently today of a world organized on a basis of beautiful, democratic principle, and while we begin to eventually realize that ideal, we must not allow ourselves to forget the great American people who we represent – a people who must have more than highly abstract phrases – a people in whom hard practicality is unwrought – such a people are ours and they are alive to the requirements of the hour, Mr President, – as much so as you and I, even though perhaps they do not handle phrases so nicely. Nor would we wish to give the conference the impression that we are forsaking our principles for the sake of expediency but we do wish the conference to know that we represent the American people who are not willing to deal in Utopianisms but who demand that we build our league and fashion out plans on the immediate conditions that now face us – conditions growing out of this war. In its last and most perfect analysis, Mr President, we hope the League of Nations will represent internationalism in its most desirable form – we trust that the nations of the world, while still possessing the nationalism that is so important a part of a nation's consciousness, will, withal, acquire that international spirit by which all their differences may be arranged. We trust, in time, to develop a nationalism of the right sort – one that possesses all the advantages of our modern nationalism – but one which places the principle of right above such ideas as "my country right or wrong." We wish a nation to be not only nationally conscious but internationally so – and to realize its duties toward its associated nations.

Please do not conceive our ideas as of the maudlin, sentimental, Bolshevist variety – it is a dream now – but we hope to make it possible by building on a rock.

And that is what we wish to do, Mr President. And that is why we will make some concessions now to Expediency at the expense of Principle for we realize, sir, that before this idea in its full conception can dominate men – a world consciousness must be evolved.

And, as the American people, are a nation of dreamers who dream from facts we will fashion our league according to the demands of the immediate present and let Lenin bring about the evolution [MS possibly incomplete].

THE CAROLINA SMOKER

With Noise Makers, Confetti, Eats and Near Artists
Annual University event under the auspices
of the Y. M. C. A.

Swain Hall, March 9th, 1920, 9 P. M.

Toastmaster, DR. COLLIER COBB

1. Piano . . . "Ikey" Brooks
2. Satyr Stunt
3. Eats
4. Jazz Band
5. Wrestling Match . Jacobi and Fulton
6. Quartette . Howell, Nichols, Brooks, Thompson
7. Eats
8. Mandolin Club
9. Co-ed Stunt
10. Eats
11. Glee Club
12. Toasts: Tom Wolfe, from Students; Dr. Moss, from Community; Dr. Chase, from University
13. Piano . . . "Ikey" Brooks
14. Grand Revue
15. Hark the Sound

No Encores

Smoker Committee: DONNELL VAN NOPPEN, Chairman; R. C. BERNAU, Assistant Chairman; Assistants: T. S. KITTRELL, H. E. FULTON, J. P. WASHBURN, J. V. BAGGETT, J. L. COBB, DR. A. S. WHEELER, W. R. WUNSCH, DR. J. M. BOOKER, T. E. RONDTHALER, BILL POINDEXTER, MISS HUGHES, JONATHAN DANIELS, MISS COBB, MISS VERNER.

Broadside. North Carolina Collection, University of North Carolina at Chapel Hill

Appendix C

Class Stunt

Wolfe collaborated on the Junior Week stunt ("Junior Week Program Never Dragged Minute Is Popular Verdict," *Tar Heel*, May 2, 1919, 1, 6). He wrote this note for the printed program, which has not been located. The four-page manuscript is in the William B. Wisdom collection, Houghton Library, Harvard University.

M.J.B.

North Carolina Collection, University of North Carolina at Chapel Hill

(of course, the above has nothing at all to do with our stunt, title, names – nothing. However, we thought it would amuse you, so we had it printed. We would like to tell you here something about our stunt, but, as a matter of fact, we know nothing about it ourselves. Therefore, dear audience, we both have something to look forward to. We are just as much interested in seeing what we can do on the spur of the moment as you are. This statement, perhaps, interests you more than our stunt will. However, the admission is small and what would one expect nowadays for a quarter ($0.25) of a dollar?

Besides, the program is yours now – you may keep it as a souvenir – do anything you like with it. That alone it worth something.

We realize, of course, that you, dear audience, use us for your own purposes and that as soon as the floor at Bynums is well waxed you will ruthlessly leave us here. Therefore, we owe you nothing. But we are determined to keep you here as long as you can stand it.

Just a word before parting; We wish to make ourselves plain. If at any time or at any place in the program we should make some such stage direction as "A year elapses between Sc. I and Sc. II" – we want you to understand this means *us* – not *you*.

You do not have to wait a year. No-No.

The Stunt Committee
(So called thru courtesy)